Thank you for choosing BOOKSZOOKA!

As a small family company, we value your opinions and advice to create better products. We hope to give all of our clients the best service possible. Please let us know about your experience working with us. Your feedback is both appreciated and helpful.

Also, we would like to hear from you and see your work:

 @BooksZooka

 BooksZooka

 hello@bookszooka.com

Date: _____ Address: _____

# THANKS FOR VISITING! PLEASE SIGN IN

Name: _____ Phone: _____

Email: _____

Favorite home feature: _____

Recommended Improvements: _____

Price Opinion: _____

How did you learn about this open house? _____

O Newspaper  O Sign  O Real Estate Agent  O Internet          O Other

Is this your first visit?                    O Yes  O No

Do you have a Realtor?  O Yes (what is his name?)              O No

Are you pre-qualified/pre-approved to buy a home?       O Yes  O No

What is your time frame for purchasing a new home? ONow OJust looking OWithin a year

Do you have a home to sell?                  O Yes  O No

Do you want us to contact you?               O Yes  O No

Please list any special needs or comments: _____

_____

Thank you for registering! Disclaimer: We will only send information related to your real estate needs.

Name: _____ Phone: _____

Email: _____

Favorite home feature: _____

Recommended Improvements: _____

Price Opinion: _____

How did you learn about this open house? _____

O Newspaper  O Sign  O Real Estate Agent  O Internet          O Other

Is this your first visit?                    O Yes  O No

Do you have a Realtor?  O Yes (what is his name?)              O No

Are you pre-qualified/pre-approved to buy a home?       O Yes  O No

What is your time frame for purchasing a new home? ONow OJust looking OWithin a year

Do you have a home to sell?                  O Yes  O No

Do you want us to contact you?               O Yes  O No

Please list any special needs or comments: _____

_____

Thank you for registering! Disclaimer: We will only send information related to your real estate needs.

Date: _____     Address: _____

# THANKS FOR VISITING! PLEASE SIGN IN

Name: _____ Phone: _____

Email: _____

Favorite home feature: _____

Recommended Improvements: _____

Price Opinion: _____

How did you learn about this open house? _____

O Newspaper  O Sign  O Real Estate Agent  O Internet                O Other

Is this your first visit?                              O Yes  O No

Do you have a Realtor?   O Yes (what is his name?)                    O No

Are you pre-qualified/pre-approved to buy a home?          O Yes  O No

What is your time frame for purchasing a new home?  ONow  OJust looking  OWithin a year

Do you have a home to sell?                            O Yes  O No

Do you want us to contact you?                         O Yes  O No

Please list any special needs or comments: _____

_____

Thank you for registering! Disclaimer: We will only send information related to your real estate needs.

Name: _____ Phone: _____

Email: _____

Favorite home feature: _____

Recommended Improvements: _____

Price Opinion: _____

How did you learn about this open house? _____

O Newspaper  O Sign  O Real Estate Agent  O Internet                O Other

Is this your first visit?                              O Yes  O No

Do you have a Realtor?   O Yes (what is his name?)                    O No

Are you pre-qualified/pre-approved to buy a home?          O Yes  O No

What is your time frame for purchasing a new home?  ONow  OJust looking  OWithin a year

Do you have a home to sell?                            O Yes  O No

Do you want us to contact you?                         O Yes  O No

Please list any special needs or comments: _____

_____

Thank you for registering! Disclaimer: We will only send information related to your real estate needs.

Date: _____ Address: _____

# THANKS FOR VISITING! PLEASE SIGN IN

Name: _____ Phone: _____

Email: _____

Favorite home feature: _____

Recommended Improvements: _____

Price Opinion: _____

How did you learn about this open house? _____

O Newspaper  O Sign  O Real Estate Agent  O Internet                    O Other

Is this your first visit?                           O Yes  O No

Do you have a Realtor?  O Yes (what is his name?)                       O No

Are you pre-qualified/pre-approved to buy a home?        O Yes  O No

What is your time frame for purchasing a new home? ONow OJust looking OWithin a year

Do you have a home to sell?                          O Yes  O No

Do you want us to contact you?                       O Yes  O No

Please list any special needs or comments: _____

_____

Thank you for registering! Disclaimer: We will only send information related to your real estate needs.

Name: _____ Phone: _____

Email: _____

Favorite home feature: _____

Recommended Improvements: _____

Price Opinion: _____

How did you learn about this open house? _____

O Newspaper  O Sign  O Real Estate Agent  O Internet                    O Other

Is this your first visit?                           O Yes  O No

Do you have a Realtor?  O Yes (what is his name?)                       O No

Are you pre-qualified/pre-approved to buy a home?        O Yes  O No

What is your time frame for purchasing a new home? ONow OJust looking OWithin a year

Do you have a home to sell?                          O Yes  O No

Do you want us to contact you?                       O Yes  O No

Please list any special needs or comments: _____

_____

Thank you for registering! Disclaimer: We will only send information related to your real estate needs.

Date: _____ Address: _____

# THANKS FOR VISITING! PLEASE SIGN IN

Name: _____ Phone: _____

Email: _____

Favorite home feature: _____

Recommended Improvements: _____

Price Opinion: _____

How did you learn about this open house? _____

O Newspaper  O Sign  O Real Estate Agent  O Internet                    O Other

Is this your first visit?                              O Yes  O No

Do you have a Realtor?  O Yes (what is his name?) _____              O No

Are you pre-qualified/pre-approved to buy a home?          O Yes  O No

What is your time frame for purchasing a new home? ONow OJust looking OWithin a year

Do you have a home to sell?                          O Yes  O No

Do you want us to contact you?                       O Yes  O No

Please list any special needs or comments: _____

_____

Thank you for registering! Disclaimer: We will only send information related to your real estate needs.

---

Name: _____ Phone: _____

Email: _____

Favorite home feature: _____

Recommended Improvements: _____

Price Opinion: _____

How did you learn about this open house? _____

O Newspaper  O Sign  O Real Estate Agent  O Internet                    O Other

Is this your first visit?                              O Yes  O No

Do you have a Realtor?  O Yes (what is his name?) _____              O No

Are you pre-qualified/pre-approved to buy a home?          O Yes  O No

What is your time frame for purchasing a new home? ONow OJust looking OWithin a year

Do you have a home to sell?                          O Yes  O No

Do you want us to contact you?                       O Yes  O No

Please list any special needs or comments: _____

_____

Thank you for registering! Disclaimer: We will only send information related to your real estate needs.

Date: _____  Address: _____

# THANKS FOR VISITING! PLEASE SIGN IN

Name: _____  Phone: _____

Email: _____

Favorite home feature: _____

Recommended Improvements: _____

Price Opinion: _____

How did you learn about this open house? _____

O Newspaper  O Sign  O Real Estate Agent  O Internet              O Other

Is this your first visit?                           O Yes  O No

Do you have a Realtor?  O Yes (what is his name?) _____      O No

Are you pre-qualified/pre-approved to buy a home?        O Yes  O No

What is your time frame for purchasing a new home?  ONow  OJust looking  OWithin a year

Do you have a home to sell?                          O Yes  O No

Do you want us to contact you?                       O Yes  O No

Please list any special needs or comments: _____

_____

_____

Thank you for registering! Disclaimer: We will only send information related to your real estate needs.

---

Name: _____  Phone: _____

Email: _____

Favorite home feature: _____

Recommended Improvements: _____

Price Opinion: _____

How did you learn about this open house? _____

O Newspaper  O Sign  O Real Estate Agent  O Internet              O Other

Is this your first visit?                           O Yes  O No

Do you have a Realtor?  O Yes (what is his name?) _____      O No

Are you pre-qualified/pre-approved to buy a home?        O Yes  O No

What is your time frame for purchasing a new home?  ONow  OJust looking  OWithin a year

Do you have a home to sell?                          O Yes  O No

Do you want us to contact you?                       O Yes  O No

Please list any special needs or comments: _____

_____

_____

Thank you for registering! Disclaimer: We will only send information related to your real estate needs.

Date: _____ Address: _____

# THANKS FOR VISITING! PLEASE SIGN IN

Name: _____ Phone: _____
Email: _____

Favorite home feature: _____
Recommended Improvements: _____
Price Opinion: _____
How did you learn about this open house? _____
O Newspaper  O Sign  O Real Estate Agent  O Internet               O Other
Is this your first visit?                    O Yes  O No
Do you have a Realtor?   O Yes (what is his name?) _____   O No
Are you pre-qualified/pre-approved to buy a home?        O Yes  O No
What is your time frame for purchasing a new home? ONow  OJust looking  OWithin a year
Do you have a home to sell?                      O Yes  O No
Do you want us to contact you?                   O Yes  O No
Please list any special needs or comments: _____
_____
_____

Thank you for registering! Disclaimer: We will only send information related to your real estate needs.

Name: _____ Phone: _____
Email: _____

Favorite home feature: _____
Recommended Improvements: _____
Price Opinion: _____
How did you learn about this open house? _____
O Newspaper  O Sign  O Real Estate Agent  O Internet               O Other
Is this your first visit?                    O Yes  O No
Do you have a Realtor?   O Yes (what is his name?) _____   O No
Are you pre-qualified/pre-approved to buy a home?        O Yes  O No
What is your time frame for purchasing a new home? ONow  OJust looking  OWithin a year
Do you have a home to sell?                      O Yes  O No
Do you want us to contact you?                   O Yes  O No
Please list any special needs or comments: _____
_____
_____

Thank you for registering! Disclaimer: We will only send information related to your real estate needs.

Date: _____   Address: _____

# THANKS FOR VISITING! PLEASE SIGN IN

Name: _____   Phone: _____

Email: _____

Favorite home feature: _____

Recommended Improvements: _____

Price Opinion: _____

How did you learn about this open house? _____

O Newspaper  O Sign  O Real Estate Agent  O Internet                    O Other

Is this your first visit?                              O Yes  O No

Do you have a Realtor?  O Yes (what is his name?) _____           O No

Are you pre-qualified/pre-approved to buy a home?        O Yes  O No

What is your time frame for purchasing a new home?  ONow  OJust looking  OWithin a year

Do you have a home to sell?                              O Yes  O No

Do you want us to contact you?                           O Yes  O No

Please list any special needs or comments: _____

_____

Thank you for registering! Disclaimer: We will only send information related to your real estate needs.

---

Name: _____   Phone: _____

Email: _____

Favorite home feature: _____

Recommended Improvements: _____

Price Opinion: _____

How did you learn about this open house? _____

O Newspaper  O Sign  O Real Estate Agent  O Internet                    O Other

Is this your first visit?                              O Yes  O No

Do you have a Realtor?  O Yes (what is his name?) _____           O No

Are you pre-qualified/pre-approved to buy a home?        O Yes  O No

What is your time frame for purchasing a new home?  ONow  OJust looking  OWithin a year

Do you have a home to sell?                              O Yes  O No

Do you want us to contact you?                           O Yes  O No

Please list any special needs or comments: _____

_____

Thank you for registering! Disclaimer: We will only send information related to your real estate needs.

Date: _____  Address: _____

# THANKS FOR VISITING! PLEASE SIGN IN

Name: _____  Phone: _____

Email: _____

Favorite home feature: _____

Recommended Improvements: _____

Price Opinion: _____

How did you learn about this open house? _____

O Newspaper  O Sign  O Real Estate Agent  O Internet          O Other

Is this your first visit?                          O Yes  O No

Do you have a Realtor?  O Yes (what is his name?)              O No

Are you pre-qualified/pre-approved to buy a home?       O Yes  O No

What is your time frame for purchasing a new home? ONow OJust looking OWithin a year

Do you have a home to sell?                     O Yes  O No

Do you want us to contact you?                  O Yes  O No

Please list any special needs or comments: _____

_____

Thank you for registering! Disclaimer: We will only send information related to your real estate needs.

---

Name: _____  Phone: _____

Email: _____

Favorite home feature: _____

Recommended Improvements: _____

Price Opinion: _____

How did you learn about this open house? _____

O Newspaper  O Sign  O Real Estate Agent  O Internet          O Other

Is this your first visit?                          O Yes  O No

Do you have a Realtor?  O Yes (what is his name?)              O No

Are you pre-qualified/pre-approved to buy a home?       O Yes  O No

What is your time frame for purchasing a new home? ONow OJust looking OWithin a year

Do you have a home to sell?                     O Yes  O No

Do you want us to contact you?                  O Yes  O No

Please list any special needs or comments: _____

_____

Thank you for registering! Disclaimer: We will only send information related to your real estate needs.

Date: _____ Address: _____

# THANKS FOR VISITING! PLEASE SIGN IN

Name: _____ Phone: _____

Email: _____

Favorite home feature: _____

Recommended Improvements: _____

Price Opinion: _____

How did you learn about this open house? _____

O Newspaper O Sign O Real Estate Agent O Internet          O Other

Is this your first visit?                    O Yes O No

Do you have a Realtor?  O Yes (what is his name?)                    O No

Are you pre-qualified/pre-approved to buy a home?          O Yes O No

What is your time frame for purchasing a new home? ONow OJust looking OWithin a year

Do you have a home to sell?                    O Yes O No

Do you want us to contact you?                    O Yes O No

Please list any special needs or comments: _____

_____

Thank you for registering! Disclaimer: We will only send information related to your real estate needs.

---

Name: _____ Phone: _____

Email: _____

Favorite home feature: _____

Recommended Improvements: _____

Price Opinion: _____

How did you learn about this open house? _____

O Newspaper O Sign O Real Estate Agent O Internet          O Other

Is this your first visit?                    O Yes O No

Do you have a Realtor?  O Yes (what is his name?)                    O No

Are you pre-qualified/pre-approved to buy a home?          O Yes O No

What is your time frame for purchasing a new home? ONow OJust looking OWithin a year

Do you have a home to sell?                    O Yes O No

Do you want us to contact you?                    O Yes O No

Please list any special needs or comments: _____

_____

Thank you for registering! Disclaimer: We will only send information related to your real estate needs.

Date: _____ Address: _____

# THANKS FOR VISITING! PLEASE SIGN IN

Name: _____ Phone: _____

Email: _____

Favorite home feature: _____

Recommended Improvements: _____

Price Opinion: _____

How did you learn about this open house? _____

O Newspaper  O Sign  O Real Estate Agent  O Internet            O Other

Is this your first visit?                    O Yes  O No

Do you have a Realtor?  O Yes (what is his name?)                    O No

Are you pre-qualified/pre-approved to buy a home?        O Yes  O No

What is your time frame for purchasing a new home? ONow OJust looking OWithin a year

Do you have a home to sell?                    O Yes  O No

Do you want us to contact you?                    O Yes  O No

Please list any special needs or comments: _____

_____

Thank you for registering! Disclaimer: We will only send information related to your real estate needs.

---

Name: _____ Phone: _____

Email: _____

Favorite home feature: _____

Recommended Improvements: _____

Price Opinion: _____

How did you learn about this open house? _____

O Newspaper  O Sign  O Real Estate Agent  O Internet            O Other

Is this your first visit?                    O Yes  O No

Do you have a Realtor?  O Yes (what is his name?)                    O No

Are you pre-qualified/pre-approved to buy a home?        O Yes  O No

What is your time frame for purchasing a new home? ONow OJust looking OWithin a year

Do you have a home to sell?                    O Yes  O No

Do you want us to contact you?                    O Yes  O No

Please list any special needs or comments: _____

_____

Thank you for registering! Disclaimer: We will only send information related to your real estate needs.

Date: _____ Address: _____

# THANKS FOR VISITING! PLEASE SIGN IN

Name: _____ Phone: _____

Email: _____

Favorite home feature: _____

Recommended Improvements: _____

Price Opinion: _____

How did you learn about this open house? _____

O Newspaper  O Sign  O Real Estate Agent  O Internet          O Other

Is this your first visit?                        O Yes  O No

Do you have a Realtor?  O Yes (what is his name?) _____  O No

Are you pre-qualified/pre-approved to buy a home?      O Yes  O No

What is your time frame for purchasing a new home?  ONow  OJust looking  OWithin a year

Do you have a home to sell?                      O Yes  O No

Do you want us to contact you?                   O Yes  O No

Please list any special needs or comments: _____

_____

Thank you for registering! Disclaimer: We will only send information related to your real estate needs.

---

Name: _____ Phone: _____

Email: _____

Favorite home feature: _____

Recommended Improvements: _____

Price Opinion: _____

How did you learn about this open house? _____

O Newspaper  O Sign  O Real Estate Agent  O Internet          O Other

Is this your first visit?                        O Yes  O No

Do you have a Realtor?  O Yes (what is his name?) _____  O No

Are you pre-qualified/pre-approved to buy a home?      O Yes  O No

What is your time frame for purchasing a new home?  ONow  OJust looking  OWithin a year

Do you have a home to sell?                      O Yes  O No

Do you want us to contact you?                   O Yes  O No

Please list any special needs or comments: _____

_____

Thank you for registering! Disclaimer: We will only send information related to your real estate needs.

Date: _____    Address: _____

# THANKS FOR VISITING! PLEASE SIGN IN

Name: _____    Phone: _____

Email: _____

Favorite home feature: _____

Recommended Improvements: _____

Price Opinion: _____

How did you learn about this open house? _____

O Newspaper  O Sign  O Real Estate Agent  O Internet                    O Other

Is this your first visit?                                    O Yes  O No

Do you have a Realtor?   O Yes (what is his name?)                       O No

Are you pre-qualified/pre-approved to buy a home?          O Yes  O No

What is your time frame for purchasing a new home? ONow OJust looking OWithin a year

Do you have a home to sell?                                O Yes  O No

Do you want us to contact you?                             O Yes  O No

Please list any special needs or comments: _____

_____

Thank you for registering! Disclaimer: We will only send information related to your real estate needs.

---

Name: _____    Phone: _____

Email: _____

Favorite home feature: _____

Recommended Improvements: _____

Price Opinion: _____

How did you learn about this open house? _____

O Newspaper  O Sign  O Real Estate Agent  O Internet                    O Other

Is this your first visit?                                    O Yes  O No

Do you have a Realtor?   O Yes (what is his name?)                       O No

Are you pre-qualified/pre-approved to buy a home?          O Yes  O No

What is your time frame for purchasing a new home? ONow OJust looking OWithin a year

Do you have a home to sell?                                O Yes  O No

Do you want us to contact you?                             O Yes  O No

Please list any special needs or comments: _____

_____

Thank you for registering! Disclaimer: We will only send information related to your real estate needs.

Date: _____ Address: _____

# THANKS FOR VISITING! PLEASE SIGN IN

Name: _____ Phone: _____

Email: _____

Favorite home feature: _____

Recommended Improvements: _____

Price Opinion: _____

How did you learn about this open house? _____

O Newspaper  O Sign  O Real Estate Agent  O Internet                    O Other

Is this your first visit?                              O Yes  O No

Do you have a Realtor?  O Yes (what is his name?)                    O No

Are you pre-qualified/pre-approved to buy a home?        O Yes  O No

What is your time frame for purchasing a new home? ONow OJust looking OWithin a year

Do you have a home to sell?                          O Yes  O No

Do you want us to contact you?                       O Yes  O No

Please list any special needs or comments: _____

_____

Thank you for registering! Disclaimer: We will only send information related to your real estate needs.

---

Name: _____ Phone: _____

Email: _____

Favorite home feature: _____

Recommended Improvements: _____

Price Opinion: _____

How did you learn about this open house? _____

O Newspaper  O Sign  O Real Estate Agent  O Internet                    O Other

Is this your first visit?                              O Yes  O No

Do you have a Realtor?  O Yes (what is his name?)                    O No

Are you pre-qualified/pre-approved to buy a home?        O Yes  O No

What is your time frame for purchasing a new home? ONow OJust looking OWithin a year

Do you have a home to sell?                          O Yes  O No

Do you want us to contact you?                       O Yes  O No

Please list any special needs or comments: _____

_____

Thank you for registering! Disclaimer: We will only send information related to your real estate needs.

Date: _____ Address: _____

# THANKS FOR VISITING! PLEASE SIGN IN

Name: _____ Phone: _____

Email: _____

Favorite home feature: _____

Recommended Improvements: _____

Price Opinion: _____

How did you learn about this open house? _____

O Newspaper  O Sign  O Real Estate Agent  O Internet                    O Other

Is this your first visit?                              O Yes  O No

Do you have a Realtor?  O Yes (what is his name?) _____        O No

Are you pre-qualified/pre-approved to buy a home?          O Yes  O No

What is your time frame for purchasing a new home? ONow OJust looking OWithin a year

Do you have a home to sell?                              O Yes  O No

Do you want us to contact you?                          O Yes  O No

Please list any special needs or comments: _____

_____

Thank you for registering! Disclaimer: We will only send information related to your real estate needs.

---

Name: _____ Phone: _____

Email: _____

Favorite home feature: _____

Recommended Improvements: _____

Price Opinion: _____

How did you learn about this open house? _____

O Newspaper  O Sign  O Real Estate Agent  O Internet                    O Other

Is this your first visit?                              O Yes  O No

Do you have a Realtor?  O Yes (what is his name?) _____        O No

Are you pre-qualified/pre-approved to buy a home?          O Yes  O No

What is your time frame for purchasing a new home? ONow OJust looking OWithin a year

Do you have a home to sell?                              O Yes  O No

Do you want us to contact you?                          O Yes  O No

Please list any special needs or comments: _____

_____

Thank you for registering! Disclaimer: We will only send information related to your real estate needs.

Date: _____ Address: _____

# THANKS FOR VISITING! PLEASE SIGN IN

Name: _____ Phone: _____

Email: _____

Favorite home feature: _____

Recommended Improvements: _____

Price Opinion: _____

How did you learn about this open house? _____

O Newspaper  O Sign  O Real Estate Agent  O Internet          O Other

Is this your first visit?                          O Yes O No

Do you have a Realtor?  O Yes (what is his name?)_____ O No

Are you pre-qualified/pre-approved to buy a home?      O Yes O No

What is your time frame for purchasing a new home? ONow OJust looking OWithin a year

Do you have a home to sell?                        O Yes O No

Do you want us to contact you?                     O Yes O No

Please list any special needs or comments: _____

_____

Thank you for registering! Disclaimer: We will only send information related to your real estate needs.

---

Name: _____ Phone: _____

Email: _____

Favorite home feature: _____

Recommended Improvements: _____

Price Opinion: _____

How did you learn about this open house? _____

O Newspaper  O Sign  O Real Estate Agent  O Internet          O Other

Is this your first visit?                          O Yes O No

Do you have a Realtor?  O Yes (what is his name?)_____ O No

Are you pre-qualified/pre-approved to buy a home?      O Yes O No

What is your time frame for purchasing a new home? ONow OJust looking OWithin a year

Do you have a home to sell?                        O Yes O No

Do you want us to contact you?                     O Yes O No

Please list any special needs or comments: _____

_____

Thank you for registering! Disclaimer: We will only send information related to your real estate needs.

Date: _____  Address: _____

# THANKS FOR VISITING! PLEASE SIGN IN

Name: _____  Phone: _____

Email: _____

Favorite home feature: _____

Recommended Improvements: _____

Price Opinion: _____

How did you learn about this open house? _____

O Newspaper  O Sign  O Real Estate Agent  O Internet     O Other

Is this your first visit?                    O Yes  O No

Do you have a Realtor?  O Yes (what is his name?) _____        O No

Are you pre-qualified/pre-approved to buy a home?     O Yes  O No

What is your time frame for purchasing a new home? ONow  OJust looking  OWithin a year

Do you have a home to sell?                   O Yes  O No

Do you want us to contact you?                O Yes  O No

Please list any special needs or comments: _____

_____

Thank you for registering! Disclaimer: We will only send information related to your real estate needs.

---

Name: _____  Phone: _____

Email: _____

Favorite home feature: _____

Recommended Improvements: _____

Price Opinion: _____

How did you learn about this open house? _____

O Newspaper  O Sign  O Real Estate Agent  O Internet     O Other

Is this your first visit?                    O Yes  O No

Do you have a Realtor?  O Yes (what is his name?) _____        O No

Are you pre-qualified/pre-approved to buy a home?     O Yes  O No

What is your time frame for purchasing a new home? ONow  OJust looking  OWithin a year

Do you have a home to sell?                   O Yes  O No

Do you want us to contact you?                O Yes  O No

Please list any special needs or comments: _____

_____

Thank you for registering! Disclaimer: We will only send information related to your real estate needs.

Date: _____ Address: _____

# THANKS FOR VISITING! PLEASE SIGN IN

Name: _____ Phone: _____

Email: _____

Favorite home feature: _____

Recommended Improvements: _____

Price Opinion: _____

How did you learn about this open house? _____

O Newspaper  O Sign  O Real Estate Agent  O Internet                    O Other

Is this your first visit?                              O Yes  O No

Do you have a Realtor?  O Yes (what is his name?)                    O No

Are you pre-qualified/pre-approved to buy a home?         O Yes  O No

What is your time frame for purchasing a new home? ONow OJust looking OWithin a year

Do you have a home to sell?                              O Yes  O No

Do you want us to contact you?                           O Yes  O No

Please list any special needs or comments: _____

_____

_____

Thank you for registering! Disclaimer: We will only send information related to your real estate needs.

---

Name: _____ Phone: _____

Email: _____

Favorite home feature: _____

Recommended Improvements: _____

Price Opinion: _____

How did you learn about this open house? _____

O Newspaper  O Sign  O Real Estate Agent  O Internet                    O Other

Is this your first visit?                              O Yes  O No

Do you have a Realtor?  O Yes (what is his name?)                    O No

Are you pre-qualified/pre-approved to buy a home?         O Yes  O No

What is your time frame for purchasing a new home? ONow OJust looking OWithin a year

Do you have a home to sell?                              O Yes  O No

Do you want us to contact you?                           O Yes  O No

Please list any special needs or comments: _____

_____

_____

Thank you for registering! Disclaimer: We will only send information related to your real estate needs.

Date: _____ Address: _____

# THANKS FOR VISITING! PLEASE SIGN IN

Name: _____ Phone: _____

Email: _____

Favorite home feature: _____

Recommended Improvements: _____

Price Opinion: _____

How did you learn about this open house? _____

O Newspaper  O Sign  O Real Estate Agent  O Internet                    O Other

Is this your first visit?                              O Yes  O No

Do you have a Realtor?  O Yes (what is his name?) _____      O No

Are you pre-qualified/pre-approved to buy a home?        O Yes  O No

What is your time frame for purchasing a new home?  ONow  OJust looking  OWithin a year

Do you have a home to sell?                           O Yes  O No

Do you want us to contact you?                        O Yes  O No

Please list any special needs or comments: _____

_____

Thank you for registering! Disclaimer: We will only send information related to your real estate needs.

---

Name: _____ Phone: _____

Email: _____

Favorite home feature: _____

Recommended Improvements: _____

Price Opinion: _____

How did you learn about this open house? _____

O Newspaper  O Sign  O Real Estate Agent  O Internet                    O Other

Is this your first visit?                              O Yes  O No

Do you have a Realtor?  O Yes (what is his name?) _____      O No

Are you pre-qualified/pre-approved to buy a home?        O Yes  O No

What is your time frame for purchasing a new home?  ONow  OJust looking  OWithin a year

Do you have a home to sell?                           O Yes  O No

Do you want us to contact you?                        O Yes  O No

Please list any special needs or comments: _____

_____

Thank you for registering! Disclaimer: We will only send information related to your real estate needs.

Date: _____ Address: _____

# THANKS FOR VISITING! PLEASE SIGN IN

Name: _____ Phone: _____

Email: _____

Favorite home feature: _____

Recommended Improvements: _____

Price Opinion: _____

How did you learn about this open house? _____

O Newspaper O Sign O Real Estate Agent O Internet     O Other

Is this your first visit?     O Yes O No

Do you have a Realtor? O Yes (what is his name?) _____ O No

Are you pre-qualified/pre-approved to buy a home?    O Yes O No

What is your time frame for purchasing a new home? ONow OJust looking OWithin a year

Do you have a home to sell?     O Yes O No

Do you want us to contact you?     O Yes O No

Please list any special needs or comments: _____

_____

Thank you for registering! Disclaimer: We will only send information related to your real estate needs.

---

Name: _____ Phone: _____

Email: _____

Favorite home feature: _____

Recommended Improvements: _____

Price Opinion: _____

How did you learn about this open house? _____

O Newspaper O Sign O Real Estate Agent O Internet     O Other

Is this your first visit?     O Yes O No

Do you have a Realtor? O Yes (what is his name?) _____ O No

Are you pre-qualified/pre-approved to buy a home?    O Yes O No

What is your time frame for purchasing a new home? ONow OJust looking OWithin a year

Do you have a home to sell?     O Yes O No

Do you want us to contact you?     O Yes O No

Please list any special needs or comments: _____

_____

Thank you for registering! Disclaimer: We will only send information related to your real estate needs.

Date: _____ Address: _____

# THANKS FOR VISITING! PLEASE SIGN IN

Name: _____ Phone: _____

Email: _____

Favorite home feature: _____

Recommended Improvements: _____

Price Opinion: _____

How did you learn about this open house? _____

O Newspaper  O Sign  O Real Estate Agent  O Internet          O Other

Is this your first visit?                    O Yes  O No

Do you have a Realtor?  O Yes (what is his name?)              O No

Are you pre-qualified/pre-approved to buy a home?      O Yes  O No

What is your time frame for purchasing a new home? ONow OJust looking OWithin a year

Do you have a home to sell?                  O Yes  O No

Do you want us to contact you?               O Yes  O No

Please list any special needs or comments: _____

_____

Thank you for registering! Disclaimer: We will only send information related to your real estate needs.

Name: _____ Phone: _____

Email: _____

Favorite home feature: _____

Recommended Improvements: _____

Price Opinion: _____

How did you learn about this open house? _____

O Newspaper  O Sign  O Real Estate Agent  O Internet          O Other

Is this your first visit?                    O Yes  O No

Do you have a Realtor?  O Yes (what is his name?)              O No

Are you pre-qualified/pre-approved to buy a home?      O Yes  O No

What is your time frame for purchasing a new home? ONow OJust looking OWithin a year

Do you have a home to sell?                  O Yes  O No

Do you want us to contact you?               O Yes  O No

Please list any special needs or comments: _____

_____

Thank you for registering! Disclaimer: We will only send information related to your real estate needs.

Date: _____ Address: _____

# THANKS FOR VISITING! PLEASE SIGN IN

Name: _____ Phone: _____

Email: _____

Favorite home feature: _____

Recommended Improvements: _____

Price Opinion: _____

How did you learn about this open house? _____

O Newspaper O Sign O Real Estate Agent O Internet          O Other

Is this your first visit?                              O Yes O No

Do you have a Realtor? O Yes (what is his name?)               O No

Are you pre-qualified/pre-approved to buy a home?      O Yes O No

What is your time frame for purchasing a new home? ONow OJust looking OWithin a year

Do you have a home to sell?                           O Yes O No

Do you want us to contact you?                        O Yes O No

Please list any special needs or comments: _____

_____

Thank you for registering! Disclaimer: We will only send information related to your real estate needs.

Name: _____ Phone: _____

Email: _____

Favorite home feature: _____

Recommended Improvements: _____

Price Opinion: _____

How did you learn about this open house? _____

O Newspaper O Sign O Real Estate Agent O Internet          O Other

Is this your first visit?                              O Yes O No

Do you have a Realtor? O Yes (what is his name?)               O No

Are you pre-qualified/pre-approved to buy a home?      O Yes O No

What is your time frame for purchasing a new home? ONow OJust looking OWithin a year

Do you have a home to sell?                           O Yes O No

Do you want us to contact you?                        O Yes O No

Please list any special needs or comments: _____

_____

Thank you for registering! Disclaimer: We will only send information related to your real estate needs.

Date: _____ Address: _____

# THANKS FOR VISITING! PLEASE SIGN IN

Name: _____ Phone: _____

Email: _____

Favorite home feature: _____

Recommended Improvements: _____

Price Opinion: _____

How did you learn about this open house? _____

O Newspaper  O Sign  O Real Estate Agent  O Internet            O Other

Is this your first visit?                          O Yes  O No

Do you have a Realtor?  O Yes (what is his name?) _____  O No

Are you pre-qualified/pre-approved to buy a home?      O Yes  O No

What is your time frame for purchasing a new home?  ONow  OJust looking  OWithin a year

Do you have a home to sell?                        O Yes  O No

Do you want us to contact you?                     O Yes  O No

Please list any special needs or comments: _____

_____

Thank you for registering! Disclaimer: We will only send information related to your real estate needs.

---

Name: _____ Phone: _____

Email: _____

Favorite home feature: _____

Recommended Improvements: _____

Price Opinion: _____

How did you learn about this open house? _____

O Newspaper  O Sign  O Real Estate Agent  O Internet            O Other

Is this your first visit?                          O Yes  O No

Do you have a Realtor?  O Yes (what is his name?) _____  O No

Are you pre-qualified/pre-approved to buy a home?      O Yes  O No

What is your time frame for purchasing a new home?  ONow  OJust looking  OWithin a year

Do you have a home to sell?                        O Yes  O No

Do you want us to contact you?                     O Yes  O No

Please list any special needs or comments: _____

_____

Thank you for registering! Disclaimer: We will only send information related to your real estate needs.

Date: _____ Address: _____

# THANKS FOR VISITING! PLEASE SIGN IN

Name: _____ Phone: _____

Email: _____

Favorite home feature: _____

Recommended Improvements: _____

Price Opinion: _____

How did you learn about this open house? _____

O Newspaper  O Sign  O Real Estate Agent  O Internet          O Other

Is this your first visit?                    O Yes  O No

Do you have a Realtor?  O Yes (what is his name?) _____    O No

Are you pre-qualified/pre-approved to buy a home?   O Yes  O No

What is your time frame for purchasing a new home? ONow OJust looking OWithin a year

Do you have a home to sell?                  O Yes  O No

Do you want us to contact you?               O Yes  O No

Please list any special needs or comments: _____

_____

Thank you for registering! Disclaimer: We will only send information related to your real estate needs.

Name: _____ Phone: _____

Email: _____

Favorite home feature: _____

Recommended Improvements: _____

Price Opinion: _____

How did you learn about this open house? _____

O Newspaper  O Sign  O Real Estate Agent  O Internet          O Other

Is this your first visit?                    O Yes  O No

Do you have a Realtor?  O Yes (what is his name?) _____    O No

Are you pre-qualified/pre-approved to buy a home?   O Yes  O No

What is your time frame for purchasing a new home? ONow OJust looking OWithin a year

Do you have a home to sell?                  O Yes  O No

Do you want us to contact you?               O Yes  O No

Please list any special needs or comments: _____

_____

Thank you for registering! Disclaimer: We will only send information related to your real estate needs.

Date: _____  Address: _____

# THANKS FOR VISITING! PLEASE SIGN IN

Name: _____ Phone: _____
Email: _____

Favorite home feature: _____
Recommended Improvements: _____
Price Opinion: _____
How did you learn about this open house? _____
O Newspaper  O Sign  O Real Estate Agent  O Internet              O Other
Is this your first visit?                    O Yes  O No
Do you have a Realtor?  O Yes (what is his name?)                  O No
Are you pre-qualified/pre-approved to buy a home?        O Yes  O No
What is your time frame for purchasing a new home? ONow OJust looking OWithin a year
Do you have a home to sell?                     O Yes  O No
Do you want us to contact you?                  O Yes  O No
Please list any special needs or comments: _____
_____

Thank you for registering! Disclaimer: We will only send information related to your real estate needs.

Name: _____ Phone: _____
Email: _____

Favorite home feature: _____
Recommended Improvements: _____
Price Opinion: _____
How did you learn about this open house? _____
O Newspaper  O Sign  O Real Estate Agent  O Internet              O Other
Is this your first visit?                    O Yes  O No
Do you have a Realtor?  O Yes (what is his name?)                  O No
Are you pre-qualified/pre-approved to buy a home?        O Yes  O No
What is your time frame for purchasing a new home? ONow OJust looking OWithin a year
Do you have a home to sell?                     O Yes  O No
Do you want us to contact you?                  O Yes  O No
Please list any special needs or comments: _____
_____

Thank you for registering! Disclaimer: We will only send information related to your real estate needs.

Date: _____ Address: _____

# THANKS FOR VISITING! PLEASE SIGN IN

Name: _____ Phone: _____

Email: _____

Favorite home feature: _____

Recommended Improvements: _____

Price Opinion: _____

How did you learn about this open house? _____

O Newspaper  O Sign  O Real Estate Agent  O Internet                    O Other

Is this your first visit?                              O Yes  O No

Do you have a Realtor?  O Yes (what is his name?)                        O No

Are you pre-qualified/pre-approved to buy a home?        O Yes  O No

What is your time frame for purchasing a new home?  ONow OJust looking OWithin a year

Do you have a home to sell?                              O Yes  O No

Do you want us to contact you?                           O Yes  O No

Please list any special needs or comments: _____

_____

Thank you for registering! Disclaimer: We will only send information related to your real estate needs.

---

Name: _____ Phone: _____

Email: _____

Favorite home feature: _____

Recommended Improvements: _____

Price Opinion: _____

How did you learn about this open house? _____

O Newspaper  O Sign  O Real Estate Agent  O Internet                    O Other

Is this your first visit?                              O Yes  O No

Do you have a Realtor?  O Yes (what is his name?)                        O No

Are you pre-qualified/pre-approved to buy a home?        O Yes  O No

What is your time frame for purchasing a new home?  ONow OJust looking OWithin a year

Do you have a home to sell?                              O Yes  O No

Do you want us to contact you?                           O Yes  O No

Please list any special needs or comments: _____

_____

Thank you for registering! Disclaimer: We will only send information related to your real estate needs.

Date: _____ Address: _____

# THANKS FOR VISITING! PLEASE SIGN IN

Name: _____ Phone: _____

Email: _____

Favorite home feature: _____

Recommended Improvements: _____

Price Opinion: _____

How did you learn about this open house? _____

O Newspaper  O Sign  O Real Estate Agent  O Internet                O Other

Is this your first visit?                        O Yes  O No

Do you have a Realtor?  O Yes (what is his name?) _____        O No

Are you pre-qualified/pre-approved to buy a home?        O Yes  O No

What is your time frame for purchasing a new home? ONow OJust looking OWithin a year

Do you have a home to sell?                      O Yes  O No

Do you want us to contact you?                   O Yes  O No

Please list any special needs or comments: _____

_____

Thank you for registering! Disclaimer: We will only send information related to your real estate needs.

---

Name: _____ Phone: _____

Email: _____

Favorite home feature: _____

Recommended Improvements: _____

Price Opinion: _____

How did you learn about this open house? _____

O Newspaper  O Sign  O Real Estate Agent  O Internet                O Other

Is this your first visit?                        O Yes  O No

Do you have a Realtor?  O Yes (what is his name?) _____        O No

Are you pre-qualified/pre-approved to buy a home?        O Yes  O No

What is your time frame for purchasing a new home? ONow OJust looking OWithin a year

Do you have a home to sell?                      O Yes  O No

Do you want us to contact you?                   O Yes  O No

Please list any special needs or comments: _____

_____

Thank you for registering! Disclaimer: We will only send information related to your real estate needs.

Date: _____ Address: _____

# THANKS FOR VISITING! PLEASE SIGN IN

Name: _____ Phone: _____

Email: _____

Favorite home feature: _____

Recommended Improvements: _____

Price Opinion: _____

How did you learn about this open house? _____

O Newspaper  O Sign  O Real Estate Agent  O Internet          O Other

Is this your first visit?                              O Yes  O No

Do you have a Realtor?  O Yes (what is his name?) _____        O No

Are you pre-qualified/pre-approved to buy a home?      O Yes  O No

What is your time frame for purchasing a new home?  ONow  OJust looking  OWithin a year

Do you have a home to sell?                            O Yes  O No

Do you want us to contact you?                         O Yes  O No

Please list any special needs or comments: _____

_____

Thank you for registering! Disclaimer: We will only send information related to your real estate needs.

---

Name: _____ Phone: _____

Email: _____

Favorite home feature: _____

Recommended Improvements: _____

Price Opinion: _____

How did you learn about this open house? _____

O Newspaper  O Sign  O Real Estate Agent  O Internet          O Other

Is this your first visit?                              O Yes  O No

Do you have a Realtor?  O Yes (what is his name?) _____        O No

Are you pre-qualified/pre-approved to buy a home?      O Yes  O No

What is your time frame for purchasing a new home?  ONow  OJust looking  OWithin a year

Do you have a home to sell?                            O Yes  O No

Do you want us to contact you?                         O Yes  O No

Please list any special needs or comments: _____

_____

Thank you for registering! Disclaimer: We will only send information related to your real estate needs.

Date: _____ Address: _____

# THANKS FOR VISITING! PLEASE SIGN IN

Name: _____ Phone: _____

Email: _____

Favorite home feature: _____

Recommended Improvements: _____

Price Opinion: _____

How did you learn about this open house? _____

O Newspaper  O Sign  O Real Estate Agent  O Internet                    O Other

Is this your first visit?                                    O Yes  O No

Do you have a Realtor?   O Yes (what is his name?) _____ O No

Are you pre-qualified/pre-approved to buy a home?            O Yes  O No

What is your time frame for purchasing a new home? ONow  OJust looking  OWithin a year

Do you have a home to sell?                                  O Yes  O No

Do you want us to contact you?                               O Yes  O No

Please list any special needs or comments: _____

_____

Thank you for registering! Disclaimer: We will only send information related to your real estate needs.

---

Name: _____ Phone: _____

Email: _____

Favorite home feature: _____

Recommended Improvements: _____

Price Opinion: _____

How did you learn about this open house? _____

O Newspaper  O Sign  O Real Estate Agent  O Internet                    O Other

Is this your first visit?                                    O Yes  O No

Do you have a Realtor?   O Yes (what is his name?) _____ O No

Are you pre-qualified/pre-approved to buy a home?            O Yes  O No

What is your time frame for purchasing a new home? ONow  OJust looking  OWithin a year

Do you have a home to sell?                                  O Yes  O No

Do you want us to contact you?                               O Yes  O No

Please list any special needs or comments: _____

_____

Thank you for registering! Disclaimer: We will only send information related to your real estate needs.

Date: _____ Address: _____

# THANKS FOR VISITING! PLEASE SIGN IN

Name: _____ Phone: _____

Email: _____

Favorite home feature: _____

Recommended Improvements: _____

Price Opinion: _____

How did you learn about this open house? _____

O Newspaper O Sign O Real Estate Agent O Internet      O Other

Is this your first visit?      O Yes O No

Do you have a Realtor?   O Yes (what is his name?)      O No

Are you pre-qualified/pre-approved to buy a home?      O Yes O No

What is your time frame for purchasing a new home? ONow OJust looking OWithin a year

Do you have a home to sell?      O Yes O No

Do you want us to contact you?      O Yes O No

Please list any special needs or comments: _____

_____

_____

Thank you for registering! Disclaimer: We will only send information related to your real estate needs.

---

Name: _____ Phone: _____

Email: _____

Favorite home feature: _____

Recommended Improvements: _____

Price Opinion: _____

How did you learn about this open house? _____

O Newspaper O Sign O Real Estate Agent O Internet      O Other

Is this your first visit?      O Yes O No

Do you have a Realtor?   O Yes (what is his name?)      O No

Are you pre-qualified/pre-approved to buy a home?      O Yes O No

What is your time frame for purchasing a new home? ONow OJust looking OWithin a year

Do you have a home to sell?      O Yes O No

Do you want us to contact you?      O Yes O No

Please list any special needs or comments: _____

_____

_____

Thank you for registering! Disclaimer: We will only send information related to your real estate needs.

Date: _____ Address: _____

# THANKS FOR VISITING! PLEASE SIGN IN

Name: _____ Phone: _____

Email: _____

Favorite home feature: _____

Recommended Improvements: _____

Price Opinion: _____

How did you learn about this open house? _____

O Newspaper O Sign O Real Estate Agent O Internet          O Other

Is this your first visit?                    O Yes O No

Do you have a Realtor?  O Yes (what is his name?) _____     O No

Are you pre-qualified/pre-approved to buy a home?      O Yes O No

What is your time frame for purchasing a new home? ONow OJust looking OWithin a year

Do you have a home to sell?                    O Yes O No

Do you want us to contact you?                 O Yes O No

Please list any special needs or comments: _____

_____

Thank you for registering! Disclaimer: We will only send information related to your real estate needs.

---

Name: _____ Phone: _____

Email: _____

Favorite home feature: _____

Recommended Improvements: _____

Price Opinion: _____

How did you learn about this open house? _____

O Newspaper O Sign O Real Estate Agent O Internet          O Other

Is this your first visit?                    O Yes O No

Do you have a Realtor?  O Yes (what is his name?) _____     O No

Are you pre-qualified/pre-approved to buy a home?      O Yes O No

What is your time frame for purchasing a new home? ONow OJust looking OWithin a year

Do you have a home to sell?                    O Yes O No

Do you want us to contact you?                 O Yes O No

Please list any special needs or comments: _____

_____

Thank you for registering! Disclaimer: We will only send information related to your real estate needs.

Date: _____ Address: _____

# THANKS FOR VISITING! PLEASE SIGN IN

Name: _____ Phone: _____

Email: _____

Favorite home feature: _____

Recommended Improvements: _____

Price Opinion: _____

How did you learn about this open house? _____

O Newspaper  O Sign  O Real Estate Agent  O Internet          O Other

Is this your first visit?                        O Yes  O No

Do you have a Realtor?  O Yes (what is his name?) _____  O No

Are you pre-qualified/pre-approved to buy a home?        O Yes  O No

What is your time frame for purchasing a new home? ONow OJust looking OWithin a year

Do you have a home to sell?                      O Yes  O No

Do you want us to contact you?                   O Yes  O No

Please list any special needs or comments: _____

_____

Thank you for registering! Disclaimer: We will only send information related to your real estate needs.

---

Name: _____ Phone: _____

Email: _____

Favorite home feature: _____

Recommended Improvements: _____

Price Opinion: _____

How did you learn about this open house? _____

O Newspaper  O Sign  O Real Estate Agent  O Internet          O Other

Is this your first visit?                        O Yes  O No

Do you have a Realtor?  O Yes (what is his name?) _____  O No

Are you pre-qualified/pre-approved to buy a home?        O Yes  O No

What is your time frame for purchasing a new home? ONow OJust looking OWithin a year

Do you have a home to sell?                      O Yes  O No

Do you want us to contact you?                   O Yes  O No

Please list any special needs or comments: _____

_____

Thank you for registering! Disclaimer: We will only send information related to your real estate needs.

Date: _____ Address: _____

# THANKS FOR VISITING! PLEASE SIGN IN

Name: _____ Phone: _____

Email: _____

Favorite home feature: _____

Recommended Improvements: _____

Price Opinion: _____

How did you learn about this open house? _____

O Newspaper  O Sign  O Real Estate Agent  O Internet          O Other

Is this your first visit?                                  O Yes  O No

Do you have a Realtor?  O Yes (what is his name?)                    O No

Are you pre-qualified/pre-approved to buy a home?         O Yes  O No

What is your time frame for purchasing a new home? ONow OJust looking OWithin a year

Do you have a home to sell?                               O Yes  O No

Do you want us to contact you?                            O Yes  O No

Please list any special needs or comments: _____

_____

Thank you for registering! Disclaimer: We will only send information related to your real estate needs.

---

Name: _____ Phone: _____

Email: _____

Favorite home feature: _____

Recommended Improvements: _____

Price Opinion: _____

How did you learn about this open house? _____

O Newspaper  O Sign  O Real Estate Agent  O Internet          O Other

Is this your first visit?                                  O Yes  O No

Do you have a Realtor?  O Yes (what is his name?)                    O No

Are you pre-qualified/pre-approved to buy a home?         O Yes  O No

What is your time frame for purchasing a new home? ONow OJust looking OWithin a year

Do you have a home to sell?                               O Yes  O No

Do you want us to contact you?                            O Yes  O No

Please list any special needs or comments: _____

_____

Thank you for registering! Disclaimer: We will only send information related to your real estate needs.

Date: _____ Address: _____

# THANKS FOR VISITING! PLEASE SIGN IN

---

Name: _____ Phone: _____

Email: _____

Favorite home feature: _____

Recommended Improvements: _____

Price Opinion: _____

How did you learn about this open house? _____

O Newspaper  O Sign  O Real Estate Agent  O Internet          O Other

Is this your first visit?                          O Yes  O No

Do you have a Realtor?  O Yes (what is his name?)                O No

Are you pre-qualified/pre-approved to buy a home?      O Yes  O No

What is your time frame for purchasing a new home? ONow OJust looking OWithin a year

Do you have a home to sell?                         O Yes  O No

Do you want us to contact you?                      O Yes  O No

Please list any special needs or comments: _____

_____

Thank you for registering! Disclaimer: We will only send information related to your real estate needs.

---

Name: _____ Phone: _____

Email: _____

Favorite home feature: _____

Recommended Improvements: _____

Price Opinion: _____

How did you learn about this open house? _____

O Newspaper  O Sign  O Real Estate Agent  O Internet          O Other

Is this your first visit?                          O Yes  O No

Do you have a Realtor?  O Yes (what is his name?)                O No

Are you pre-qualified/pre-approved to buy a home?      O Yes  O No

What is your time frame for purchasing a new home? ONow OJust looking OWithin a year

Do you have a home to sell?                         O Yes  O No

Do you want us to contact you?                      O Yes  O No

Please list any special needs or comments: _____

_____

Thank you for registering! Disclaimer: We will only send information related to your real estate needs.

Date: _____ Address: _____

# THANKS FOR VISITING! PLEASE SIGN IN

Name: _____ Phone: _____

Email: _____

Favorite home feature: _____

Recommended Improvements: _____

Price Opinion: _____

How did you learn about this open house? _____

O Newspaper  O Sign  O Real Estate Agent  O Internet                    O Other

Is this your first visit?                                    O Yes  O No

Do you have a Realtor?  O Yes (what is his name?)                        O No

Are you pre-qualified/pre-approved to buy a home?          O Yes  O No

What is your time frame for purchasing a new home?  ONow  OJust looking  OWithin a year

Do you have a home to sell?                                O Yes  O No

Do you want us to contact you?                             O Yes  O No

Please list any special needs or comments: _____

_____

Thank you for registering! Disclaimer: We will only send information related to your real estate needs.

---

Name: _____ Phone: _____

Email: _____

Favorite home feature: _____

Recommended Improvements: _____

Price Opinion: _____

How did you learn about this open house? _____

O Newspaper  O Sign  O Real Estate Agent  O Internet                    O Other

Is this your first visit?                                    O Yes  O No

Do you have a Realtor?  O Yes (what is his name?)                        O No

Are you pre-qualified/pre-approved to buy a home?          O Yes  O No

What is your time frame for purchasing a new home?  ONow  OJust looking  OWithin a year

Do you have a home to sell?                                O Yes  O No

Do you want us to contact you?                             O Yes  O No

Please list any special needs or comments: _____

_____

Thank you for registering! Disclaimer: We will only send information related to your real estate needs.

Date: _____  Address: _____

# THANKS FOR VISITING! PLEASE SIGN IN

Name: _____  Phone: _____

Email: _____

Favorite home feature: _____

Recommended Improvements: _____

Price Opinion: _____

How did you learn about this open house? _____

O Newspaper  O Sign  O Real Estate Agent  O Internet        O Other

Is this your first visit?                          O Yes  O No

Do you have a Realtor?  O Yes (what is his name?) _____  O No

Are you pre-qualified/pre-approved to buy a home?        O Yes  O No

What is your time frame for purchasing a new home?  ONow  OJust looking  OWithin a year

Do you have a home to sell?                         O Yes  O No

Do you want us to contact you?                      O Yes  O No

Please list any special needs or comments: _____

_____

Thank you for registering! Disclaimer: We will only send information related to your real estate needs.

---

Name: _____  Phone: _____

Email: _____

Favorite home feature: _____

Recommended Improvements: _____

Price Opinion: _____

How did you learn about this open house? _____

O Newspaper  O Sign  O Real Estate Agent  O Internet        O Other

Is this your first visit?                          O Yes  O No

Do you have a Realtor?  O Yes (what is his name?) _____  O No

Are you pre-qualified/pre-approved to buy a home?        O Yes  O No

What is your time frame for purchasing a new home?  ONow  OJust looking  OWithin a year

Do you have a home to sell?                         O Yes  O No

Do you want us to contact you?                      O Yes  O No

Please list any special needs or comments: _____

_____

Thank you for registering! Disclaimer: We will only send information related to your real estate needs.

Date: _____    Address: _____

# THANKS FOR VISITING! PLEASE SIGN IN

Name: _____    Phone: _____

Email: _____

Favorite home feature: _____

Recommended Improvements: _____

Price Opinion: _____

How did you learn about this open house? _____

O Newspaper  O Sign  O Real Estate Agent  O Internet          O Other

Is this your first visit?                    O Yes  O No

Do you have a Realtor?  O Yes (what is his name?)                    O No

Are you pre-qualified/pre-approved to buy a home?        O Yes  O No

What is your time frame for purchasing a new home? ONow OJust looking OWithin a year

Do you have a home to sell?                    O Yes  O No

Do you want us to contact you?                    O Yes  O No

Please list any special needs or comments: _____

_____

Thank you for registering! Disclaimer: We will only send information related to your real estate needs.

Name: _____    Phone: _____

Email: _____

Favorite home feature: _____

Recommended Improvements: _____

Price Opinion: _____

How did you learn about this open house? _____

O Newspaper  O Sign  O Real Estate Agent  O Internet          O Other

Is this your first visit?                    O Yes  O No

Do you have a Realtor?  O Yes (what is his name?)                    O No

Are you pre-qualified/pre-approved to buy a home?        O Yes  O No

What is your time frame for purchasing a new home? ONow OJust looking OWithin a year

Do you have a home to sell?                    O Yes  O No

Do you want us to contact you?                    O Yes  O No

Please list any special needs or comments: _____

_____

Thank you for registering! Disclaimer: We will only send information related to your real estate needs.

Date: _____ Address: _____

# THANKS FOR VISITING! PLEASE SIGN IN

Name: _____ Phone: _____

Email: _____

Favorite home feature: _____

Recommended Improvements: _____

Price Opinion: _____

How did you learn about this open house? _____

O Newspaper  O Sign  O Real Estate Agent  O Internet                    O Other

Is this your first visit?                          O Yes  O No

Do you have a Realtor?  O Yes (what is his name?)                         O No

Are you pre-qualified/pre-approved to buy a home?        O Yes  O No

What is your time frame for purchasing a new home?  ONow  OJust looking  OWithin a year

Do you have a home to sell?                              O Yes  O No

Do you want us to contact you?                           O Yes  O No

Please list any special needs or comments: _____

_____

Thank you for registering! Disclaimer: We will only send information related to your real estate needs.

---

Name: _____ Phone: _____

Email: _____

Favorite home feature: _____

Recommended Improvements: _____

Price Opinion: _____

How did you learn about this open house? _____

O Newspaper  O Sign  O Real Estate Agent  O Internet                    O Other

Is this your first visit?                          O Yes  O No

Do you have a Realtor?  O Yes (what is his name?)                         O No

Are you pre-qualified/pre-approved to buy a home?        O Yes  O No

What is your time frame for purchasing a new home?  ONow  OJust looking  OWithin a year

Do you have a home to sell?                              O Yes  O No

Do you want us to contact you?                           O Yes  O No

Please list any special needs or comments: _____

_____

Thank you for registering! Disclaimer: We will only send information related to your real estate needs.

Date: _____ Address: _____

# THANKS FOR VISITING! PLEASE SIGN IN

Name: _____ Phone: _____

Email: _____

Favorite home feature: _____

Recommended Improvements: _____

Price Opinion: _____

How did you learn about this open house? _____

O Newspaper  O Sign  O Real Estate Agent  O Internet                    O Other

Is this your first visit?                              O Yes  O No

Do you have a Realtor?  O Yes (what is his name?) _____            O No

Are you pre-qualified/pre-approved to buy a home?            O Yes  O No

What is your time frame for purchasing a new home? ONow OJust looking OWithin a year

Do you have a home to sell?                              O Yes  O No

Do you want us to contact you?                           O Yes  O No

Please list any special needs or comments: _____

_____

Thank you for registering! Disclaimer: We will only send information related to your real estate needs.

Name: _____ Phone: _____

Email: _____

Favorite home feature: _____

Recommended Improvements: _____

Price Opinion: _____

How did you learn about this open house? _____

O Newspaper  O Sign  O Real Estate Agent  O Internet                    O Other

Is this your first visit?                              O Yes  O No

Do you have a Realtor?  O Yes (what is his name?) _____            O No

Are you pre-qualified/pre-approved to buy a home?            O Yes  O No

What is your time frame for purchasing a new home? ONow OJust looking OWithin a year

Do you have a home to sell?                              O Yes  O No

Do you want us to contact you?                           O Yes  O No

Please list any special needs or comments: _____

_____

Thank you for registering! Disclaimer: We will only send information related to your real estate needs.

Date: _____  Address: _____

# THANKS FOR VISITING! PLEASE SIGN IN

Name: _____  Phone: _____

Email: _____

Favorite home feature: _____

Recommended Improvements: _____

Price Opinion: _____

How did you learn about this open house? _____

O Newspaper  O Sign  O Real Estate Agent  O Internet        O Other

Is this your first visit?                              O Yes  O No

Do you have a Realtor?  O Yes (what is his name?) _____        O No

Are you pre-qualified/pre-approved to buy a home?        O Yes  O No

What is your time frame for purchasing a new home?  ONow  OJust looking  OWithin a year

Do you have a home to sell?                           O Yes  O No

Do you want us to contact you?                        O Yes  O No

Please list any special needs or comments: _____

_____

Thank you for registering! Disclaimer: We will only send information related to your real estate needs.

---

Name: _____  Phone: _____

Email: _____

Favorite home feature: _____

Recommended Improvements: _____

Price Opinion: _____

How did you learn about this open house? _____

O Newspaper  O Sign  O Real Estate Agent  O Internet        O Other

Is this your first visit?                              O Yes  O No

Do you have a Realtor?  O Yes (what is his name?) _____        O No

Are you pre-qualified/pre-approved to buy a home?        O Yes  O No

What is your time frame for purchasing a new home?  ONow  OJust looking  OWithin a year

Do you have a home to sell?                           O Yes  O No

Do you want us to contact you?                        O Yes  O No

Please list any special needs or comments: _____

_____

Thank you for registering! Disclaimer: We will only send information related to your real estate needs.

Date: _____ Address: _____

# THANKS FOR VISITING! PLEASE SIGN IN

Name: _____ Phone: _____

Email: _____

Favorite home feature: _____

Recommended Improvements: _____

Price Opinion: _____

How did you learn about this open house? _____

O Newspaper  O Sign  O Real Estate Agent  O Internet          O Other

Is this your first visit?                              O Yes  O No

Do you have a Realtor?  O Yes (what is his name?) _____  O No

Are you pre-qualified/pre-approved to buy a home?         O Yes  O No

What is your time frame for purchasing a new home? ONow  OJust looking  OWithin a year

Do you have a home to sell?                              O Yes  O No

Do you want us to contact you?                           O Yes  O No

Please list any special needs or comments: _____

_____

Thank you for registering! Disclaimer: We will only send information related to your real estate needs.

---

Name: _____ Phone: _____

Email: _____

Favorite home feature: _____

Recommended Improvements: _____

Price Opinion: _____

How did you learn about this open house? _____

O Newspaper  O Sign  O Real Estate Agent  O Internet          O Other

Is this your first visit?                              O Yes  O No

Do you have a Realtor?  O Yes (what is his name?) _____  O No

Are you pre-qualified/pre-approved to buy a home?         O Yes  O No

What is your time frame for purchasing a new home? ONow  OJust looking  OWithin a year

Do you have a home to sell?                              O Yes  O No

Do you want us to contact you?                           O Yes  O No

Please list any special needs or comments: _____

_____

Thank you for registering! Disclaimer: We will only send information related to your real estate needs.

Date: _____ Address: _____

# THANKS FOR VISITING! PLEASE SIGN IN

Name: _____ Phone: _____

Email: _____

Favorite home feature: _____

Recommended Improvements: _____

Price Opinion: _____

How did you learn about this open house? _____

O Newspaper  O Sign  O Real Estate Agent  O Internet          O Other

Is this your first visit?                                 O Yes  O No

Do you have a Realtor?  O Yes (what is his name?) _____ O No

Are you pre-qualified/pre-approved to buy a home?        O Yes  O No

What is your time frame for purchasing a new home? ONow OJust looking OWithin a year

Do you have a home to sell?                              O Yes  O No

Do you want us to contact you?                          O Yes  O No

Please list any special needs or comments: _____

_____

Thank you for registering! Disclaimer: We will only send information related to your real estate needs.

---

Name: _____ Phone: _____

Email: _____

Favorite home feature: _____

Recommended Improvements: _____

Price Opinion: _____

How did you learn about this open house? _____

O Newspaper  O Sign  O Real Estate Agent  O Internet          O Other

Is this your first visit?                                 O Yes  O No

Do you have a Realtor?  O Yes (what is his name?) _____ O No

Are you pre-qualified/pre-approved to buy a home?        O Yes  O No

What is your time frame for purchasing a new home? ONow OJust looking OWithin a year

Do you have a home to sell?                              O Yes  O No

Do you want us to contact you?                          O Yes  O No

Please list any special needs or comments: _____

_____

Thank you for registering! Disclaimer: We will only send information related to your real estate needs.

Date: _____  Address: _____

# THANKS FOR VISITING! PLEASE SIGN IN

Name: _____  Phone: _____

Email: _____

Favorite home feature: _____

Recommended Improvements: _____

Price Opinion: _____

How did you learn about this open house? _____

O Newspaper  O Sign  O Real Estate Agent  O Internet          O Other

Is this your first visit?                           O Yes  O No

Do you have a Realtor?  O Yes (what is his name?) _____          O No

Are you pre-qualified/pre-approved to buy a home?        O Yes  O No

What is your time frame for purchasing a new home? ONow OJust looking OWithin a year

Do you have a home to sell?                         O Yes  O No

Do you want us to contact you?                      O Yes  O No

Please list any special needs or comments: _____

_____

Thank you for registering! Disclaimer: We will only send information related to your real estate needs.

---

Name: _____  Phone: _____

Email: _____

Favorite home feature: _____

Recommended Improvements: _____

Price Opinion: _____

How did you learn about this open house? _____

O Newspaper  O Sign  O Real Estate Agent  O Internet          O Other

Is this your first visit?                           O Yes  O No

Do you have a Realtor?  O Yes (what is his name?) _____          O No

Are you pre-qualified/pre-approved to buy a home?        O Yes  O No

What is your time frame for purchasing a new home? ONow OJust looking OWithin a year

Do you have a home to sell?                         O Yes  O No

Do you want us to contact you?                      O Yes  O No

Please list any special needs or comments: _____

_____

Thank you for registering! Disclaimer: We will only send information related to your real estate needs.

Date: _____ Address: _____

# THANKS FOR VISITING! PLEASE SIGN IN

Name: _____ Phone: _____

Email: _____

Favorite home feature: _____

Recommended Improvements: _____

Price Opinion: _____

How did you learn about this open house? _____

O Newspaper  O Sign  O Real Estate Agent  O Internet          O Other

Is this your first visit?                    O Yes  O No

Do you have a Realtor?  O Yes (what is his name?)                    O No
_____

Are you pre-qualified/pre-approved to buy a home?     O Yes  O No

What is your time frame for purchasing a new home? ONow OJust looking OWithin a year

Do you have a home to sell?                   O Yes  O No

Do you want us to contact you?                O Yes  O No

Please list any special needs or comments: _____

_____

_____

Thank you for registering! Disclaimer: We will only send information related to your real estate needs.

---

Name: _____ Phone: _____

Email: _____

Favorite home feature: _____

Recommended Improvements: _____

Price Opinion: _____

How did you learn about this open house? _____

O Newspaper  O Sign  O Real Estate Agent  O Internet          O Other

Is this your first visit?                    O Yes  O No

Do you have a Realtor?  O Yes (what is his name?)                    O No

Are you pre-qualified/pre-approved to buy a home?     O Yes  O No

What is your time frame for purchasing a new home? ONow OJust looking OWithin a year

Do you have a home to sell?                   O Yes  O No

Do you want us to contact you?                O Yes  O No

Please list any special needs or comments: _____

_____

_____

Thank you for registering! Disclaimer: We will only send information related to your real estate needs.

Date: _____ Address: _____

# THANKS FOR VISITING! PLEASE SIGN IN

Name: _____ Phone: _____

Email: _____

Favorite home feature: _____

Recommended Improvements: _____

Price Opinion: _____

How did you learn about this open house? _____

O Newspaper  O Sign  O Real Estate Agent  O Internet          O Other

Is this your first visit?                          O Yes  O No

Do you have a Realtor?  O Yes (what is his name?)              O No

Are you pre-qualified/pre-approved to buy a home?        O Yes  O No

What is your time frame for purchasing a new home? ONow OJust looking OWithin a year

Do you have a home to sell?                         O Yes  O No

Do you want us to contact you?                      O Yes  O No

Please list any special needs or comments: _____

_____

Thank you for registering! Disclaimer: We will only send information related to your real estate needs.

---

Name: _____ Phone: _____

Email: _____

Favorite home feature: _____

Recommended Improvements: _____

Price Opinion: _____

How did you learn about this open house? _____

O Newspaper  O Sign  O Real Estate Agent  O Internet          O Other

Is this your first visit?                          O Yes  O No

Do you have a Realtor?  O Yes (what is his name?)              O No

Are you pre-qualified/pre-approved to buy a home?        O Yes  O No

What is your time frame for purchasing a new home? ONow OJust looking OWithin a year

Do you have a home to sell?                         O Yes  O No

Do you want us to contact you?                      O Yes  O No

Please list any special needs or comments: _____

_____

Thank you for registering! Disclaimer: We will only send information related to your real estate needs.

Date: _____ Address: _____

# THANKS FOR VISITING! PLEASE SIGN IN

Name: _____ Phone: _____

Email: _____

Favorite home feature: _____

Recommended Improvements: _____

Price Opinion: _____

How did you learn about this open house? _____

O Newspaper O Sign O Real Estate Agent O Internet          O Other

Is this your first visit?                              O Yes O No

Do you have a Realtor?  O Yes (what is his name?)                    O No

Are you pre-qualified/pre-approved to buy a home?        O Yes O No

What is your time frame for purchasing a new home? ONow OJust looking OWithin a year

Do you have a home to sell?                            O Yes O No

Do you want us to contact you?                         O Yes O No

Please list any special needs or comments: _____

_____

Thank you for registering! Disclaimer: We will only send information related to your real estate needs.

---

Name: _____ Phone: _____

Email: _____

Favorite home feature: _____

Recommended Improvements: _____

Price Opinion: _____

How did you learn about this open house? _____

O Newspaper O Sign O Real Estate Agent O Internet          O Other

Is this your first visit?                              O Yes O No

Do you have a Realtor?  O Yes (what is his name?)                    O No

Are you pre-qualified/pre-approved to buy a home?        O Yes O No

What is your time frame for purchasing a new home? ONow OJust looking OWithin a year

Do you have a home to sell?                            O Yes O No

Do you want us to contact you?                         O Yes O No

Please list any special needs or comments: _____

_____

Thank you for registering! Disclaimer: We will only send information related to your real estate needs.

Date: _____ Address: _____

# THANKS FOR VISITING! PLEASE SIGN IN

Name: _____ Phone: _____

Email: _____

Favorite home feature: _____

Recommended Improvements: _____

Price Opinion: _____

How did you learn about this open house? _____

O Newspaper  O Sign  O Real Estate Agent  O Internet              O Other

Is this your first visit?                              O Yes  O No

Do you have a Realtor?  O Yes (what is his name?)                  O No

Are you pre-qualified/pre-approved to buy a home?        O Yes  O No

What is your time frame for purchasing a new home?  ONow OJust looking OWithin a year

Do you have a home to sell?                              O Yes  O No

Do you want us to contact you?                          O Yes  O No

Please list any special needs or comments: _____

_____

Thank you for registering! Disclaimer: We will only send information related to your real estate needs.

---

Name: _____ Phone: _____

Email: _____

Favorite home feature: _____

Recommended Improvements: _____

Price Opinion: _____

How did you learn about this open house? _____

O Newspaper  O Sign  O Real Estate Agent  O Internet              O Other

Is this your first visit?                              O Yes  O No

Do you have a Realtor?  O Yes (what is his name?)                  O No

Are you pre-qualified/pre-approved to buy a home?        O Yes  O No

What is your time frame for purchasing a new home?  ONow OJust looking OWithin a year

Do you have a home to sell?                              O Yes  O No

Do you want us to contact you?                          O Yes  O No

Please list any special needs or comments: _____

_____

Thank you for registering! Disclaimer: We will only send information related to your real estate needs.

Date: _____ Address: _____

# THANKS FOR VISITING! PLEASE SIGN IN

Name: _____ Phone: _____

Email: _____

Favorite home feature: _____

Recommended Improvements: _____

Price Opinion: _____

How did you learn about this open house? _____

O Newspaper  O Sign  O Real Estate Agent  O Internet          O Other

Is this your first visit?                              O Yes  O No

Do you have a Realtor?  O Yes (what is his name?) _____  O No

Are you pre-qualified/pre-approved to buy a home?        O Yes  O No

What is your time frame for purchasing a new home? ONow OJust looking OWithin a year

Do you have a home to sell?                          O Yes  O No

Do you want us to contact you?                       O Yes  O No

Please list any special needs or comments: _____

_____

Thank you for registering! Disclaimer: We will only send information related to your real estate needs.

---

Name: _____ Phone: _____

Email: _____

Favorite home feature: _____

Recommended Improvements: _____

Price Opinion: _____

How did you learn about this open house? _____

O Newspaper  O Sign  O Real Estate Agent  O Internet          O Other

Is this your first visit?                              O Yes  O No

Do you have a Realtor?  O Yes (what is his name?) _____  O No

Are you pre-qualified/pre-approved to buy a home?        O Yes  O No

What is your time frame for purchasing a new home? ONow OJust looking OWithin a year

Do you have a home to sell?                          O Yes  O No

Do you want us to contact you?                       O Yes  O No

Please list any special needs or comments: _____

_____

Thank you for registering! Disclaimer: We will only send information related to your real estate needs.

Date: _____    Address: _____

# THANKS FOR VISITING! PLEASE SIGN IN

Name: _____    Phone: _____
Email: _____

Favorite home feature: _____
Recommended Improvements: _____
Price Opinion: _____
How did you learn about this open house? _____
O Newspaper  O Sign  O Real Estate Agent  O Internet                O Other
Is this your first visit?                        O Yes O No
Do you have a Realtor?   O Yes (what is his name?)                   O No
Are you pre-qualified/pre-approved to buy a home?         O Yes O No
What is your time frame for purchasing a new home? ONow OJust looking OWithin a year
Do you have a home to sell?                              O Yes O No
Do you want us to contact you?                          O Yes O No
Please list any special needs or comments: _____
_____

Thank you for registering! Disclaimer: We will only send information related to your real estate needs.

Name: _____    Phone: _____
Email: _____

Favorite home feature: _____
Recommended Improvements: _____
Price Opinion: _____
How did you learn about this open house? _____
O Newspaper  O Sign  O Real Estate Agent  O Internet                O Other
Is this your first visit?                        O Yes O No
Do you have a Realtor?   O Yes (what is his name?)                   O No
Are you pre-qualified/pre-approved to buy a home?         O Yes O No
What is your time frame for purchasing a new home? ONow OJust looking OWithin a year
Do you have a home to sell?                              O Yes O No
Do you want us to contact you?                          O Yes O No
Please list any special needs or comments: _____
_____

Thank you for registering! Disclaimer: We will only send information related to your real estate needs.

Date: _____ Address: _____

# THANKS FOR VISITING! PLEASE SIGN IN

Name: _____ Phone: _____

Email: _____

Favorite home feature: _____

Recommended Improvements: _____

Price Opinion: _____

How did you learn about this open house? _____

O Newspaper O Sign O Real Estate Agent O Internet          O Other

Is this your first visit?                              O Yes O No

Do you have a Realtor?  O Yes (what is his name?)                    O No

Are you pre-qualified/pre-approved to buy a home?          O Yes O No

What is your time frame for purchasing a new home? ONow OJust looking OWithin a year

Do you have a home to sell?                            O Yes O No

Do you want us to contact you?                         O Yes O No

Please list any special needs or comments: _____

_____

Thank you for registering! Disclaimer: We will only send information related to your real estate needs.

---

Name: _____ Phone: _____

Email: _____

Favorite home feature: _____

Recommended Improvements: _____

Price Opinion: _____

How did you learn about this open house? _____

O Newspaper O Sign O Real Estate Agent O Internet          O Other

Is this your first visit?                              O Yes O No

Do you have a Realtor?  O Yes (what is his name?)                    O No

Are you pre-qualified/pre-approved to buy a home?          O Yes O No

What is your time frame for purchasing a new home? ONow OJust looking OWithin a year

Do you have a home to sell?                            O Yes O No

Do you want us to contact you?                         O Yes O No

Please list any special needs or comments: _____

_____

Thank you for registering! Disclaimer: We will only send information related to your real estate needs.

Date: _____ Address: _____

# THANKS FOR VISITING! PLEASE SIGN IN

Name: _____ Phone: _____

Email: _____

Favorite home feature: _____

Recommended Improvements: _____

Price Opinion: _____

How did you learn about this open house? _____

O Newspaper  O Sign  O Real Estate Agent  O Internet            O Other

Is this your first visit?                         O Yes  O No

Do you have a Realtor?  O Yes (what is his name?) _____            O No

Are you pre-qualified/pre-approved to buy a home?        O Yes  O No

What is your time frame for purchasing a new home? ONow OJust looking OWithin a year

Do you have a home to sell?                         O Yes  O No

Do you want us to contact you?                         O Yes  O No

Please list any special needs or comments: _____

_____

Thank you for registering! Disclaimer: We will only send information related to your real estate needs.

---

Name: _____ Phone: _____

Email: _____

Favorite home feature: _____

Recommended Improvements: _____

Price Opinion: _____

How did you learn about this open house? _____

O Newspaper  O Sign  O Real Estate Agent  O Internet            O Other

Is this your first visit?                         O Yes  O No

Do you have a Realtor?  O Yes (what is his name?) _____            O No

Are you pre-qualified/pre-approved to buy a home?        O Yes  O No

What is your time frame for purchasing a new home? ONow OJust looking OWithin a year

Do you have a home to sell?                         O Yes  O No

Do you want us to contact you?                         O Yes  O No

Please list any special needs or comments: _____

_____

Thank you for registering! Disclaimer: We will only send information related to your real estate needs.

Date: _____ Address: _____

# THANKS FOR VISITING! PLEASE SIGN IN

Name: _____ Phone: _____

Email: _____

Favorite home feature: _____

Recommended Improvements: _____

Price Opinion: _____

How did you learn about this open house? _____

O Newspaper  O Sign  O Real Estate Agent  O Internet                O Other

Is this your first visit?                    O Yes  O No

Do you have a Realtor?  O Yes (what is his name?) _____        O No

Are you pre-qualified/pre-approved to buy a home?        O Yes  O No

What is your time frame for purchasing a new home?  ONow  OJust looking  OWithin a year

Do you have a home to sell?                    O Yes  O No

Do you want us to contact you?                    O Yes  O No

Please list any special needs or comments: _____

_____

Thank you for registering! Disclaimer: We will only send information related to your real estate needs.

---

Name: _____ Phone: _____

Email: _____

Favorite home feature: _____

Recommended Improvements: _____

Price Opinion: _____

How did you learn about this open house? _____

O Newspaper  O Sign  O Real Estate Agent  O Internet                O Other

Is this your first visit?                    O Yes  O No

Do you have a Realtor?  O Yes (what is his name?) _____        O No

Are you pre-qualified/pre-approved to buy a home?        O Yes  O No

What is your time frame for purchasing a new home?  ONow  OJust looking  OWithin a year

Do you have a home to sell?                    O Yes  O No

Do you want us to contact you?                    O Yes  O No

Please list any special needs or comments: _____

_____

Thank you for registering! Disclaimer: We will only send information related to your real estate needs.

Date: _____ Address: _____

# THANKS FOR VISITING! PLEASE SIGN IN

Name: _____ Phone: _____

Email: _____

Favorite home feature: _____

Recommended Improvements: _____

Price Opinion: _____

How did you learn about this open house? _____

O Newspaper  O Sign  O Real Estate Agent  O Internet                    O Other

Is this your first visit?                              O Yes  O No

Do you have a Realtor?  O Yes (what is his name?)                         O No

Are you pre-qualified/pre-approved to buy a home?        O Yes  O No

What is your time frame for purchasing a new home? ONow OJust looking OWithin a year

Do you have a home to sell?                            O Yes  O No

Do you want us to contact you?                         O Yes  O No

Please list any special needs or comments: _____

_____

Thank you for registering! Disclaimer: We will only send information related to your real estate needs.

---

Name: _____ Phone: _____

Email: _____

Favorite home feature: _____

Recommended Improvements: _____

Price Opinion: _____

How did you learn about this open house? _____

O Newspaper  O Sign  O Real Estate Agent  O Internet                    O Other

Is this your first visit?                              O Yes  O No

Do you have a Realtor?  O Yes (what is his name?)                         O No

Are you pre-qualified/pre-approved to buy a home?        O Yes  O No

What is your time frame for purchasing a new home? ONow OJust looking OWithin a year

Do you have a home to sell?                            O Yes  O No

Do you want us to contact you?                         O Yes  O No

Please list any special needs or comments: _____

_____

Thank you for registering! Disclaimer: We will only send information related to your real estate needs.

Date: _____ Address: _____

# THANKS FOR VISITING! PLEASE SIGN IN

Name: _____ Phone: _____

Email: _____

Favorite home feature: _____

Recommended Improvements: _____

Price Opinion: _____

How did you learn about this open house? _____

O Newspaper  O Sign  O Real Estate Agent  O Internet          O Other

Is this your first visit?                        O Yes  O No

Do you have a Realtor?  O Yes (what is his name?) _____          O No

Are you pre-qualified/pre-approved to buy a home?          O Yes  O No

What is your time frame for purchasing a new home?  ONow  OJust looking  OWithin a year

Do you have a home to sell?                      O Yes  O No

Do you want us to contact you?                   O Yes  O No

Please list any special needs or comments: _____

_____

Thank you for registering! Disclaimer: We will only send information related to your real estate needs.

---

Name: _____ Phone: _____

Email: _____

Favorite home feature: _____

Recommended Improvements: _____

Price Opinion: _____

How did you learn about this open house? _____

O Newspaper  O Sign  O Real Estate Agent  O Internet          O Other

Is this your first visit?                        O Yes  O No

Do you have a Realtor?  O Yes (what is his name?) _____          O No

Are you pre-qualified/pre-approved to buy a home?          O Yes  O No

What is your time frame for purchasing a new home?  ONow  OJust looking  OWithin a year

Do you have a home to sell?                      O Yes  O No

Do you want us to contact you?                   O Yes  O No

Please list any special needs or comments: _____

_____

Thank you for registering! Disclaimer: We will only send information related to your real estate needs.

Date: _____  Address: _____

# THANKS FOR VISITING! PLEASE SIGN IN

Name: _____ Phone: _____
Email: _____

Favorite home feature: _____
Recommended Improvements: _____
Price Opinion: _____
How did you learn about this open house? _____
O Newspaper  O Sign  O Real Estate Agent  O Internet                    O Other
Is this your first visit?                              O Yes  O No
Do you have a Realtor?  O Yes (what is his name?) _____  O No
Are you pre-qualified/pre-approved to buy a home?        O Yes  O No
What is your time frame for purchasing a new home? ONow OJust looking OWithin a year
Do you have a home to sell?                             O Yes  O No
Do you want us to contact you?                          O Yes  O No
Please list any special needs or comments: _____
_____

Thank you for registering! Disclaimer: We will only send information related to your real estate needs.

Name: _____ Phone: _____
Email: _____

Favorite home feature: _____
Recommended Improvements: _____
Price Opinion: _____
How did you learn about this open house? _____
O Newspaper  O Sign  O Real Estate Agent  O Internet                    O Other
Is this your first visit?                              O Yes  O No
Do you have a Realtor?  O Yes (what is his name?) _____  O No
Are you pre-qualified/pre-approved to buy a home?        O Yes  O No
What is your time frame for purchasing a new home? ONow OJust looking OWithin a year
Do you have a home to sell?                             O Yes  O No
Do you want us to contact you?                          O Yes  O No
Please list any special needs or comments: _____
_____

Thank you for registering! Disclaimer: We will only send information related to your real estate needs.

Date: _____ Address: _____

# THANKS FOR VISITING! PLEASE SIGN IN

Name: _____ Phone: _____

Email: _____

Favorite home feature: _____

Recommended Improvements: _____

Price Opinion: _____

How did you learn about this open house? _____

O Newspaper  O Sign  O Real Estate Agent  O Internet          O Other

Is this your first visit?                    O Yes  O No

Do you have a Realtor?  O Yes (what is his name?) _____        O No

Are you pre-qualified/pre-approved to buy a home?    O Yes  O No

What is your time frame for purchasing a new home? ONow OJust looking OWithin a year

Do you have a home to sell?                  O Yes  O No

Do you want us to contact you?               O Yes  O No

Please list any special needs or comments: _____

_____

Thank you for registering! Disclaimer: We will only send information related to your real estate needs.

---

Name: _____ Phone: _____

Email: _____

Favorite home feature: _____

Recommended Improvements: _____

Price Opinion: _____

How did you learn about this open house? _____

O Newspaper  O Sign  O Real Estate Agent  O Internet          O Other

Is this your first visit?                    O Yes  O No

Do you have a Realtor?  O Yes (what is his name?) _____        O No

Are you pre-qualified/pre-approved to buy a home?    O Yes  O No

What is your time frame for purchasing a new home? ONow OJust looking OWithin a year

Do you have a home to sell?                  O Yes  O No

Do you want us to contact you?               O Yes  O No

Please list any special needs or comments: _____

_____

Thank you for registering! Disclaimer: We will only send information related to your real estate needs.

Date: _____ Address: _____

# THANKS FOR VISITING! PLEASE SIGN IN

Name: _____ Phone: _____

Email: _____

Favorite home feature: _____

Recommended Improvements: _____

Price Opinion: _____

How did you learn about this open house? _____

O Newspaper  O Sign  O Real Estate Agent  O Internet          O Other

Is this your first visit?                              O Yes  O No

Do you have a Realtor?   O Yes (what is his name?)                 O No

Are you pre-qualified/pre-approved to buy a home?        O Yes  O No

What is your time frame for purchasing a new home? ONow OJust looking OWithin a year

Do you have a home to sell?                            O Yes  O No

Do you want us to contact you?                         O Yes  O No

Please list any special needs or comments: _____

_____

Thank you for registering! Disclaimer: We will only send information related to your real estate needs.

Name: _____ Phone: _____

Email: _____

Favorite home feature: _____

Recommended Improvements: _____

Price Opinion: _____

How did you learn about this open house? _____

O Newspaper  O Sign  O Real Estate Agent  O Internet          O Other

Is this your first visit?                              O Yes  O No

Do you have a Realtor?   O Yes (what is his name?)                 O No

Are you pre-qualified/pre-approved to buy a home?        O Yes  O No

What is your time frame for purchasing a new home? ONow OJust looking OWithin a year

Do you have a home to sell?                            O Yes  O No

Do you want us to contact you?                         O Yes  O No

Please list any special needs or comments: _____

_____

Thank you for registering! Disclaimer: We will only send information related to your real estate needs.

Date: _____ Address: _____

# THANKS FOR VISITING! PLEASE SIGN IN

Name: _____ Phone: _____

Email: _____

Favorite home feature: _____

Recommended Improvements: _____

Price Opinion: _____

How did you learn about this open house? _____

O Newspaper  O Sign  O Real Estate Agent  O Internet              O Other

Is this your first visit?                              O Yes  O No

Do you have a Realtor?  O Yes (what is his name?) _____              O No

Are you pre-qualified/pre-approved to buy a home?         O Yes  O No

What is your time frame for purchasing a new home?  ONow  OJust looking  OWithin a year

Do you have a home to sell?                           O Yes  O No

Do you want us to contact you?                        O Yes  O No

Please list any special needs or comments: _____

_____

Thank you for registering! Disclaimer: We will only send information related to your real estate needs.

---

Name: _____ Phone: _____

Email: _____

Favorite home feature: _____

Recommended Improvements: _____

Price Opinion: _____

How did you learn about this open house? _____

O Newspaper  O Sign  O Real Estate Agent  O Internet              O Other

Is this your first visit?                              O Yes  O No

Do you have a Realtor?  O Yes (what is his name?) _____              O No

Are you pre-qualified/pre-approved to buy a home?         O Yes  O No

What is your time frame for purchasing a new home?  ONow  OJust looking  OWithin a year

Do you have a home to sell?                           O Yes  O No

Do you want us to contact you?                        O Yes  O No

Please list any special needs or comments: _____

_____

Thank you for registering! Disclaimer: We will only send information related to your real estate needs.

Date: _____ Address: _____

# THANKS FOR VISITING! PLEASE SIGN IN

Name: _____ Phone: _____

Email: _____

Favorite home feature: _____

Recommended Improvements: _____

Price Opinion: _____

How did you learn about this open house? _____

O Newspaper  O Sign  O Real Estate Agent  O Internet          O Other

Is this your first visit?                    O Yes  O No

Do you have a Realtor?  O Yes (what is his name?) _____          O No

Are you pre-qualified/pre-approved to buy a home?        O Yes  O No

What is your time frame for purchasing a new home? ONow OJust looking OWithin a year

Do you have a home to sell?                   O Yes  O No

Do you want us to contact you?                O Yes  O No

Please list any special needs or comments: _____

_____

Thank you for registering! Disclaimer: We will only send information related to your real estate needs.

Name: _____ Phone: _____

Email: _____

Favorite home feature: _____

Recommended Improvements: _____

Price Opinion: _____

How did you learn about this open house? _____

O Newspaper  O Sign  O Real Estate Agent  O Internet          O Other

Is this your first visit?                    O Yes  O No

Do you have a Realtor?  O Yes (what is his name?) _____          O No

Are you pre-qualified/pre-approved to buy a home?        O Yes  O No

What is your time frame for purchasing a new home? ONow OJust looking OWithin a year

Do you have a home to sell?                   O Yes  O No

Do you want us to contact you?                O Yes  O No

Please list any special needs or comments: _____

_____

Thank you for registering! Disclaimer: We will only send information related to your real estate needs.

Date: _____ Address: _____

# THANKS FOR VISITING! PLEASE SIGN IN

Name: _____ Phone: _____

Email: _____

Favorite home feature: _____

Recommended Improvements: _____

Price Opinion: _____

How did you learn about this open house? _____

O Newspaper  O Sign  O Real Estate Agent  O Internet          O Other

Is this your first visit?                          O Yes  O No

Do you have a Realtor?  O Yes (what is his name?) _____          O No

Are you pre-qualified/pre-approved to buy a home?        O Yes  O No

What is your time frame for purchasing a new home? ONow OJust looking OWithin a year

Do you have a home to sell?                        O Yes  O No

Do you want us to contact you?                     O Yes  O No

Please list any special needs or comments: _____

_____

Thank you for registering! Disclaimer: We will only send information related to your real estate needs.

Name: _____ Phone: _____

Email: _____

Favorite home feature: _____

Recommended Improvements: _____

Price Opinion: _____

How did you learn about this open house? _____

O Newspaper  O Sign  O Real Estate Agent  O Internet          O Other

Is this your first visit?                          O Yes  O No

Do you have a Realtor?  O Yes (what is his name?) _____          O No

Are you pre-qualified/pre-approved to buy a home?        O Yes  O No

What is your time frame for purchasing a new home? ONow OJust looking OWithin a year

Do you have a home to sell?                        O Yes  O No

Do you want us to contact you?                     O Yes  O No

Please list any special needs or comments: _____

_____

Thank you for registering! Disclaimer: We will only send information related to your real estate needs.

Date: _____ Address: _____

# THANKS FOR VISITING! PLEASE SIGN IN

Name: _____ Phone: _____

Email: _____

Favorite home feature: _____

Recommended Improvements: _____

Price Opinion: _____

How did you learn about this open house? _____

O Newspaper  O Sign  O Real Estate Agent  O Internet          O Other

Is this your first visit?                         O Yes  O No

Do you have a Realtor?  O Yes (what is his name?) _____  O No

Are you pre-qualified/pre-approved to buy a home?       O Yes  O No

What is your time frame for purchasing a new home? ONow OJust looking OWithin a year

Do you have a home to sell?                       O Yes  O No

Do you want us to contact you?                    O Yes  O No

Please list any special needs or comments: _____

_____

Thank you for registering! Disclaimer: We will only send information related to your real estate needs.

---

Name: _____ Phone: _____

Email: _____

Favorite home feature: _____

Recommended Improvements: _____

Price Opinion: _____

How did you learn about this open house? _____

O Newspaper  O Sign  O Real Estate Agent  O Internet          O Other

Is this your first visit?                         O Yes  O No

Do you have a Realtor?  O Yes (what is his name?) _____  O No

Are you pre-qualified/pre-approved to buy a home?       O Yes  O No

What is your time frame for purchasing a new home? ONow OJust looking OWithin a year

Do you have a home to sell?                       O Yes  O No

Do you want us to contact you?                    O Yes  O No

Please list any special needs or comments: _____

_____

Thank you for registering! Disclaimer: We will only send information related to your real estate needs.

Date: _____ Address: _____

# THANKS FOR VISITING! PLEASE SIGN IN

Name: _____ Phone: _____

Email: _____

Favorite home feature: _____

Recommended Improvements: _____

Price Opinion: _____

How did you learn about this open house? _____

O Newspaper  O Sign  O Real Estate Agent  O Internet          O Other

Is this your first visit?                          O Yes  O No

Do you have a Realtor?  O Yes (what is his name?)                    O No

Are you pre-qualified/pre-approved to buy a home?       O Yes  O No

What is your time frame for purchasing a new home? ONow OJust looking OWithin a year

Do you have a home to sell?                         O Yes  O No

Do you want us to contact you?                      O Yes  O No

Please list any special needs or comments: _____

_____

Thank you for registering! Disclaimer: We will only send information related to your real estate needs.

---

Name: _____ Phone: _____

Email: _____

Favorite home feature: _____

Recommended Improvements: _____

Price Opinion: _____

How did you learn about this open house? _____

O Newspaper  O Sign  O Real Estate Agent  O Internet          O Other

Is this your first visit?                          O Yes  O No

Do you have a Realtor?  O Yes (what is his name?)                    O No

Are you pre-qualified/pre-approved to buy a home?       O Yes  O No

What is your time frame for purchasing a new home? ONow OJust looking OWithin a year

Do you have a home to sell?                         O Yes  O No

Do you want us to contact you?                      O Yes  O No

Please list any special needs or comments: _____

_____

Thank you for registering! Disclaimer: We will only send information related to your real estate needs.

Date: _____ Address: _____

# THANKS FOR VISITING! PLEASE SIGN IN

Name: _____ Phone: _____

Email: _____

Favorite home feature: _____

Recommended Improvements: _____

Price Opinion: _____

How did you learn about this open house? _____

O Newspaper  O Sign  O Real Estate Agent  O Internet          O Other

Is this your first visit?                          O Yes  O No

Do you have a Realtor?  O Yes (what is his name?) _____  O No

Are you pre-qualified/pre-approved to buy a home?        O Yes  O No

What is your time frame for purchasing a new home? ONow OJust looking OWithin a year

Do you have a home to sell?                      O Yes  O No

Do you want us to contact you?                   O Yes  O No

Please list any special needs or comments: _____

_____

Thank you for registering! Disclaimer: We will only send information related to your real estate needs.

---

Name: _____ Phone: _____

Email: _____

Favorite home feature: _____

Recommended Improvements: _____

Price Opinion: _____

How did you learn about this open house? _____

O Newspaper  O Sign  O Real Estate Agent  O Internet          O Other

Is this your first visit?                          O Yes  O No

Do you have a Realtor?  O Yes (what is his name?) _____  O No

Are you pre-qualified/pre-approved to buy a home?        O Yes  O No

What is your time frame for purchasing a new home? ONow OJust looking OWithin a year

Do you have a home to sell?                      O Yes  O No

Do you want us to contact you?                   O Yes  O No

Please list any special needs or comments: _____

_____

Thank you for registering! Disclaimer: We will only send information related to your real estate needs.

Date: _____ Address: _____

# THANKS FOR VISITING! PLEASE SIGN IN

Name: _____ Phone: _____

Email: _____

Favorite home feature: _____

Recommended Improvements: _____

Price Opinion: _____

How did you learn about this open house? _____

O Newspaper  O Sign  O Real Estate Agent  O Internet          O Other

Is this your first visit?                              O Yes  O No

Do you have a Realtor?  O Yes (what is his name?)              O No

Are you pre-qualified/pre-approved to buy a home?        O Yes  O No

What is your time frame for purchasing a new home? ONow OJust looking OWithin a year

Do you have a home to sell?                          O Yes  O No

Do you want us to contact you?                       O Yes  O No

Please list any special needs or comments: _____

_____

Thank you for registering! Disclaimer: We will only send information related to your real estate needs.

---

Name: _____ Phone: _____

Email: _____

Favorite home feature: _____

Recommended Improvements: _____

Price Opinion: _____

How did you learn about this open house? _____

O Newspaper  O Sign  O Real Estate Agent  O Internet          O Other

Is this your first visit?                              O Yes  O No

Do you have a Realtor?  O Yes (what is his name?)              O No

Are you pre-qualified/pre-approved to buy a home?        O Yes  O No

What is your time frame for purchasing a new home? ONow OJust looking OWithin a year

Do you have a home to sell?                          O Yes  O No

Do you want us to contact you?                       O Yes  O No

Please list any special needs or comments: _____

_____

Thank you for registering! Disclaimer: We will only send information related to your real estate needs.

Date: _____  Address: _____

# THANKS FOR VISITING! PLEASE SIGN IN

Name: _____  Phone: _____

Email: _____

Favorite home feature: _____

Recommended Improvements: _____

Price Opinion: _____

How did you learn about this open house? _____

O Newspaper  O Sign  O Real Estate Agent  O Internet          O Other

Is this your first visit?                              O Yes  O No

Do you have a Realtor?  O Yes (what is his name?) _____  O No

Are you pre-qualified/pre-approved to buy a home?          O Yes  O No

What is your time frame for purchasing a new home? ONow OJust looking OWithin a year

Do you have a home to sell?                           O Yes  O No

Do you want us to contact you?                        O Yes  O No

Please list any special needs or comments: _____

_____

Thank you for registering! Disclaimer: We will only send information related to your real estate needs.

---

Name: _____  Phone: _____

Email: _____

Favorite home feature: _____

Recommended Improvements: _____

Price Opinion: _____

How did you learn about this open house? _____

O Newspaper  O Sign  O Real Estate Agent  O Internet          O Other

Is this your first visit?                              O Yes  O No

Do you have a Realtor?  O Yes (what is his name?) _____  O No

Are you pre-qualified/pre-approved to buy a home?          O Yes  O No

What is your time frame for purchasing a new home? ONow OJust looking OWithin a year

Do you have a home to sell?                           O Yes  O No

Do you want us to contact you?                        O Yes  O No

Please list any special needs or comments: _____

_____

Thank you for registering! Disclaimer: We will only send information related to your real estate needs.

Date: _____ Address: _____

# THANKS FOR VISITING! PLEASE SIGN IN

Name: _____ Phone: _____

Email: _____

Favorite home feature: _____

Recommended Improvements: _____

Price Opinion: _____

How did you learn about this open house? _____

O Newspaper O Sign O Real Estate Agent O Internet          O Other

Is this your first visit?                          O Yes O No

Do you have a Realtor?  O Yes (what is his name?)                    O No

Are you pre-qualified/pre-approved to buy a home?        O Yes O No

What is your time frame for purchasing a new home? ONow OJust looking OWithin a year

Do you have a home to sell?                        O Yes O No

Do you want us to contact you?                     O Yes O No

Please list any special needs or comments: _____

_____

Thank you for registering! Disclaimer: We will only send information related to your real estate needs.

Name: _____ Phone: _____

Email: _____

Favorite home feature: _____

Recommended Improvements: _____

Price Opinion: _____

How did you learn about this open house? _____

O Newspaper O Sign O Real Estate Agent O Internet          O Other

Is this your first visit?                          O Yes O No

Do you have a Realtor?  O Yes (what is his name?)                    O No

Are you pre-qualified/pre-approved to buy a home?        O Yes O No

What is your time frame for purchasing a new home? ONow OJust looking OWithin a year

Do you have a home to sell?                        O Yes O No

Do you want us to contact you?                     O Yes O No

Please list any special needs or comments: _____

_____

Thank you for registering! Disclaimer: We will only send information related to your real estate needs.

Date: _____  Address: _____

# THANKS FOR VISITING! PLEASE SIGN IN

Name: _____  Phone: _____

Email: _____

Favorite home feature: _____

Recommended Improvements: _____

Price Opinion: _____

How did you learn about this open house? _____

O Newspaper  O Sign  O Real Estate Agent  O Internet           O Other

Is this your first visit?                    O Yes  O No

Do you have a Realtor?  O Yes (what is his name?) _____  O No

Are you pre-qualified/pre-approved to buy a home?      O Yes  O No

What is your time frame for purchasing a new home? ONow OJust looking OWithin a year

Do you have a home to sell?                  O Yes  O No

Do you want us to contact you?               O Yes  O No

Please list any special needs or comments: _____

_____

Thank you for registering! Disclaimer: We will only send information related to your real estate needs.

Name: _____  Phone: _____

Email: _____

Favorite home feature: _____

Recommended Improvements: _____

Price Opinion: _____

How did you learn about this open house? _____

O Newspaper  O Sign  O Real Estate Agent  O Internet           O Other

Is this your first visit?                    O Yes  O No

Do you have a Realtor?  O Yes (what is his name?) _____  O No

Are you pre-qualified/pre-approved to buy a home?      O Yes  O No

What is your time frame for purchasing a new home? ONow OJust looking OWithin a year

Do you have a home to sell?                  O Yes  O No

Do you want us to contact you?               O Yes  O No

Please list any special needs or comments: _____

_____

Thank you for registering! Disclaimer: We will only send information related to your real estate needs.

Date: _____ Address: _____

# THANKS FOR VISITING! PLEASE SIGN IN

Name: _____ Phone: _____

Email: _____

Favorite home feature: _____

Recommended Improvements: _____

Price Opinion: _____

How did you learn about this open house? _____

O Newspaper  O Sign  O Real Estate Agent  O Internet          O Other

Is this your first visit?                              O Yes  O No

Do you have a Realtor?  O Yes (what is his name?) _____  O No

Are you pre-qualified/pre-approved to buy a home?        O Yes  O No

What is your time frame for purchasing a new home?  ONow  OJust looking  OWithin a year

Do you have a home to sell?                           O Yes  O No

Do you want us to contact you?                        O Yes  O No

Please list any special needs or comments: _____

_____

Thank you for registering! Disclaimer: We will only send information related to your real estate needs.

Name: _____ Phone: _____

Email: _____

Favorite home feature: _____

Recommended Improvements: _____

Price Opinion: _____

How did you learn about this open house? _____

O Newspaper  O Sign  O Real Estate Agent  O Internet          O Other

Is this your first visit?                              O Yes  O No

Do you have a Realtor?  O Yes (what is his name?) _____  O No

Are you pre-qualified/pre-approved to buy a home?        O Yes  O No

What is your time frame for purchasing a new home?  ONow  OJust looking  OWithin a year

Do you have a home to sell?                           O Yes  O No

Do you want us to contact you?                        O Yes  O No

Please list any special needs or comments: _____

_____

Thank you for registering! Disclaimer: We will only send information related to your real estate needs.

Date: _____ Address: _____

# THANKS FOR VISITING! PLEASE SIGN IN

Name: _____ Phone: _____

Email: _____

Favorite home feature: _____

Recommended Improvements: _____

Price Opinion: _____

How did you learn about this open house? _____

O Newspaper  O Sign  O Real Estate Agent  O Internet                    O Other

Is this your first visit?                    O Yes  O No

Do you have a Realtor?  O Yes (what is his name?) _____        O No

Are you pre-qualified/pre-approved to buy a home?        O Yes  O No

What is your time frame for purchasing a new home? ONow OJust looking OWithin a year

Do you have a home to sell?                    O Yes  O No

Do you want us to contact you?                 O Yes  O No

Please list any special needs or comments: _____

_____

Thank you for registering! Disclaimer: We will only send information related to your real estate needs.

---

Name: _____ Phone: _____

Email: _____

Favorite home feature: _____

Recommended Improvements: _____

Price Opinion: _____

How did you learn about this open house? _____

O Newspaper  O Sign  O Real Estate Agent  O Internet                    O Other

Is this your first visit?                    O Yes  O No

Do you have a Realtor?  O Yes (what is his name?) _____        O No

Are you pre-qualified/pre-approved to buy a home?        O Yes  O No

What is your time frame for purchasing a new home? ONow OJust looking OWithin a year

Do you have a home to sell?                    O Yes  O No

Do you want us to contact you?                 O Yes  O No

Please list any special needs or comments: _____

_____

Thank you for registering! Disclaimer: We will only send information related to your real estate needs.

Date: _____ Address: _____

# THANKS FOR VISITING! PLEASE SIGN IN

Name: _____ Phone: _____

Email: _____

Favorite home feature: _____

Recommended Improvements: _____

Price Opinion: _____

How did you learn about this open house? _____

O Newspaper  O Sign  O Real Estate Agent  O Internet          O Other

Is this your first visit?                    O Yes  O No

Do you have a Realtor?  O Yes (what is his name?) _____        O No

Are you pre-qualified/pre-approved to buy a home?      O Yes  O No

What is your time frame for purchasing a new home?  ONow  OJust looking  OWithin a year

Do you have a home to sell?                   O Yes  O No

Do you want us to contact you?                O Yes  O No

Please list any special needs or comments: _____

_____

Thank you for registering! Disclaimer: We will only send information related to your real estate needs.

---

Name: _____ Phone: _____

Email: _____

Favorite home feature: _____

Recommended Improvements: _____

Price Opinion: _____

How did you learn about this open house? _____

O Newspaper  O Sign  O Real Estate Agent  O Internet          O Other

Is this your first visit?                    O Yes  O No

Do you have a Realtor?  O Yes (what is his name?) _____        O No

Are you pre-qualified/pre-approved to buy a home?      O Yes  O No

What is your time frame for purchasing a new home?  ONow  OJust looking  OWithin a year

Do you have a home to sell?                   O Yes  O No

Do you want us to contact you?                O Yes  O No

Please list any special needs or comments: _____

_____

Thank you for registering! Disclaimer: We will only send information related to your real estate needs.

Date: _____ Address: _____

# THANKS FOR VISITING! PLEASE SIGN IN

Name: _____ Phone: _____

Email: _____

Favorite home feature: _____

Recommended Improvements: _____

Price Opinion: _____

How did you learn about this open house? _____

O Newspaper  O Sign  O Real Estate Agent  O Internet          O Other

Is this your first visit?                              O Yes  O No

Do you have a Realtor?  O Yes (what is his name?) _____       O No

Are you pre-qualified/pre-approved to buy a home?          O Yes  O No

What is your time frame for purchasing a new home? ONow OJust looking OWithin a year

Do you have a home to sell?                        O Yes  O No

Do you want us to contact you?                     O Yes  O No

Please list any special needs or comments: _____

_____

Thank you for registering! Disclaimer: We will only send information related to your real estate needs.

---

Name: _____ Phone: _____

Email: _____

Favorite home feature: _____

Recommended Improvements: _____

Price Opinion: _____

How did you learn about this open house? _____

O Newspaper  O Sign  O Real Estate Agent  O Internet          O Other

Is this your first visit?                              O Yes  O No

Do you have a Realtor?  O Yes (what is his name?) _____       O No

Are you pre-qualified/pre-approved to buy a home?          O Yes  O No

What is your time frame for purchasing a new home? ONow OJust looking OWithin a year

Do you have a home to sell?                        O Yes  O No

Do you want us to contact you?                     O Yes  O No

Please list any special needs or comments: _____

_____

Thank you for registering! Disclaimer: We will only send information related to your real estate needs.

Date: _____ Address: _____

# THANKS FOR VISITING! PLEASE SIGN IN

Name: _____ Phone: _____

Email: _____

Favorite home feature: _____

Recommended Improvements: _____

Price Opinion: _____

How did you learn about this open house? _____

O Newspaper  O Sign  O Real Estate Agent  O Internet          O Other

Is this your first visit?                    O Yes  O No

Do you have a Realtor?  O Yes (what is his name?) _____  O No

Are you pre-qualified/pre-approved to buy a home?        O Yes  O No

What is your time frame for purchasing a new home? ONow OJust looking OWithin a year

Do you have a home to sell?                              O Yes  O No

Do you want us to contact you?                           O Yes  O No

Please list any special needs or comments: _____

_____

Thank you for registering! Disclaimer: We will only send information related to your real estate needs.

---

Name: _____ Phone: _____

Email: _____

Favorite home feature: _____

Recommended Improvements: _____

Price Opinion: _____

How did you learn about this open house? _____

O Newspaper  O Sign  O Real Estate Agent  O Internet          O Other

Is this your first visit?                    O Yes  O No

Do you have a Realtor?  O Yes (what is his name?) _____  O No

Are you pre-qualified/pre-approved to buy a home?        O Yes  O No

What is your time frame for purchasing a new home? ONow OJust looking OWithin a year

Do you have a home to sell?                              O Yes  O No

Do you want us to contact you?                           O Yes  O No

Please list any special needs or comments: _____

_____

Thank you for registering! Disclaimer: We will only send information related to your real estate needs.

Date: _____ Address: _____

# THANKS FOR VISITING! PLEASE SIGN IN

Name: _____ Phone: _____

Email: _____

Favorite home feature: _____

Recommended Improvements: _____

Price Opinion: _____

How did you learn about this open house? _____

O Newspaper  O Sign  O Real Estate Agent  O Internet          O Other

Is this your first visit?                    O Yes  O No

Do you have a Realtor?  O Yes (what is his name?) _____          O No

Are you pre-qualified/pre-approved to buy a home?          O Yes  O No

What is your time frame for purchasing a new home? ONow OJust looking OWithin a year

Do you have a home to sell?                    O Yes  O No

Do you want us to contact you?                    O Yes  O No

Please list any special needs or comments: _____

_____

Thank you for registering! Disclaimer: We will only send information related to your real estate needs.

Name: _____ Phone: _____

Email: _____

Favorite home feature: _____

Recommended Improvements: _____

Price Opinion: _____

How did you learn about this open house? _____

O Newspaper  O Sign  O Real Estate Agent  O Internet          O Other

Is this your first visit?                    O Yes  O No

Do you have a Realtor?  O Yes (what is his name?) _____          O No

Are you pre-qualified/pre-approved to buy a home?          O Yes  O No

What is your time frame for purchasing a new home? ONow OJust looking OWithin a year

Do you have a home to sell?                    O Yes  O No

Do you want us to contact you?                    O Yes  O No

Please list any special needs or comments: _____

_____

Thank you for registering! Disclaimer: We will only send information related to your real estate needs.

Date: _____ Address: _____

# THANKS FOR VISITING! PLEASE SIGN IN

Name: _____ Phone: _____

Email: _____

Favorite home feature: _____

Recommended Improvements: _____

Price Opinion: _____

How did you learn about this open house? _____

O Newspaper  O Sign  O Real Estate Agent  O Internet        O Other

Is this your first visit?                    O Yes  O No

Do you have a Realtor?  O Yes (what is his name?)            O No

Are you pre-qualified/pre-approved to buy a home?     O Yes  O No

What is your time frame for purchasing a new home? ONow OJust looking OWithin a year

Do you have a home to sell?                           O Yes  O No

Do you want us to contact you?                        O Yes  O No

Please list any special needs or comments: _____

_____

Thank you for registering! Disclaimer: We will only send information related to your real estate needs.

---

Name: _____ Phone: _____

Email: _____

Favorite home feature: _____

Recommended Improvements: _____

Price Opinion: _____

How did you learn about this open house? _____

O Newspaper  O Sign  O Real Estate Agent  O Internet        O Other

Is this your first visit?                    O Yes  O No

Do you have a Realtor?  O Yes (what is his name?)            O No

Are you pre-qualified/pre-approved to buy a home?     O Yes  O No

What is your time frame for purchasing a new home? ONow OJust looking OWithin a year

Do you have a home to sell?                           O Yes  O No

Do you want us to contact you?                        O Yes  O No

Please list any special needs or comments: _____

_____

Thank you for registering! Disclaimer: We will only send information related to your real estate needs.

Date: _____ Address: _____

# THANKS FOR VISITING! PLEASE SIGN IN

Name: _____ Phone: _____

Email: _____

Favorite home feature: _____

Recommended Improvements: _____

Price Opinion: _____

How did you learn about this open house? _____

O Newspaper  O Sign  O Real Estate Agent  O Internet              O Other

Is this your first visit?                              O Yes  O No

Do you have a Realtor?  O Yes (what is his name?) _____      O No

Are you pre-qualified/pre-approved to buy a home?        O Yes  O No

What is your time frame for purchasing a new home?  ONow  OJust looking  OWithin a year

Do you have a home to sell?                              O Yes  O No

Do you want us to contact you?                           O Yes  O No

Please list any special needs or comments: _____

_____

Thank you for registering! Disclaimer: We will only send information related to your real estate needs.

---

Name: _____ Phone: _____

Email: _____

Favorite home feature: _____

Recommended Improvements: _____

Price Opinion: _____

How did you learn about this open house? _____

O Newspaper  O Sign  O Real Estate Agent  O Internet              O Other

Is this your first visit?                              O Yes  O No

Do you have a Realtor?  O Yes (what is his name?) _____      O No

Are you pre-qualified/pre-approved to buy a home?        O Yes  O No

What is your time frame for purchasing a new home?  ONow  OJust looking  OWithin a year

Do you have a home to sell?                              O Yes  O No

Do you want us to contact you?                           O Yes  O No

Please list any special needs or comments: _____

_____

Thank you for registering! Disclaimer: We will only send information related to your real estate needs.

Date: _____ Address: _____

# THANKS FOR VISITING! PLEASE SIGN IN

Name: _____ Phone: _____

Email: _____

Favorite home feature: _____

Recommended Improvements: _____

Price Opinion: _____

How did you learn about this open house? _____

O Newspaper  O Sign  O Real Estate Agent  O Internet          O Other

Is this your first visit?                          O Yes  O No

Do you have a Realtor?  O Yes (what is his name?)                O No

Are you pre-qualified/pre-approved to buy a home?      O Yes  O No

What is your time frame for purchasing a new home? ONow OJust looking OWithin a year

Do you have a home to sell?                        O Yes  O No

Do you want us to contact you?                     O Yes  O No

Please list any special needs or comments: _____

_____

Thank you for registering! Disclaimer: We will only send information related to your real estate needs.

---

Name: _____ Phone: _____

Email: _____

Favorite home feature: _____

Recommended Improvements: _____

Price Opinion: _____

How did you learn about this open house? _____

O Newspaper  O Sign  O Real Estate Agent  O Internet          O Other

Is this your first visit?                          O Yes  O No

Do you have a Realtor?  O Yes (what is his name?)                O No

Are you pre-qualified/pre-approved to buy a home?      O Yes  O No

What is your time frame for purchasing a new home? ONow OJust looking OWithin a year

Do you have a home to sell?                        O Yes  O No

Do you want us to contact you?                     O Yes  O No

Please list any special needs or comments: _____

_____

Thank you for registering! Disclaimer: We will only send information related to your real estate needs.

Date: _____ Address: _____

# THANKS FOR VISITING! PLEASE SIGN IN

Name: _____ Phone: _____

Email: _____

Favorite home feature: _____

Recommended Improvements: _____

Price Opinion: _____

How did you learn about this open house? _____

O Newspaper  O Sign  O Real Estate Agent  O Internet          O Other

Is this your first visit?                    O Yes  O No

Do you have a Realtor?  O Yes (what is his name?)             O No

Are you pre-qualified/pre-approved to buy a home?        O Yes  O No

What is your time frame for purchasing a new home? ONow OJust looking OWithin a year

Do you have a home to sell?                    O Yes  O No

Do you want us to contact you?                 O Yes  O No

Please list any special needs or comments: _____

_____

Thank you for registering! Disclaimer: We will only send information related to your real estate needs.

Name: _____ Phone: _____

Email: _____

Favorite home feature: _____

Recommended Improvements: _____

Price Opinion: _____

How did you learn about this open house? _____

O Newspaper  O Sign  O Real Estate Agent  O Internet          O Other

Is this your first visit?                    O Yes  O No

Do you have a Realtor?  O Yes (what is his name?)             O No

Are you pre-qualified/pre-approved to buy a home?        O Yes  O No

What is your time frame for purchasing a new home? ONow OJust looking OWithin a year

Do you have a home to sell?                    O Yes  O No

Do you want us to contact you?                 O Yes  O No

Please list any special needs or comments: _____

_____

Thank you for registering! Disclaimer: We will only send information related to your real estate needs.

Date: _____ Address: _____

# THANKS FOR VISITING! PLEASE SIGN IN

Name: _____ Phone: _____

Email: _____

Favorite home feature: _____

Recommended Improvements: _____

Price Opinion: _____

How did you learn about this open house? _____

O Newspaper  O Sign  O Real Estate Agent  O Internet          O Other

Is this your first visit?                    O Yes  O No

Do you have a Realtor?  O Yes (what is his name?)              O No

Are you pre-qualified/pre-approved to buy a home?        O Yes  O No

What is your time frame for purchasing a new home?  ONow  OJust looking  OWithin a year

Do you have a home to sell?                  O Yes  O No

Do you want us to contact you?               O Yes  O No

Please list any special needs or comments: _____

_____

Thank you for registering! Disclaimer: We will only send information related to your real estate needs.

---

Name: _____ Phone: _____

Email: _____

Favorite home feature: _____

Recommended Improvements: _____

Price Opinion: _____

How did you learn about this open house? _____

O Newspaper  O Sign  O Real Estate Agent  O Internet          O Other

Is this your first visit?                    O Yes  O No

Do you have a Realtor?  O Yes (what is his name?)              O No

Are you pre-qualified/pre-approved to buy a home?        O Yes  O No

What is your time frame for purchasing a new home?  ONow  OJust looking  OWithin a year

Do you have a home to sell?                  O Yes  O No

Do you want us to contact you?               O Yes  O No

Please list any special needs or comments: _____

_____

Thank you for registering! Disclaimer: We will only send information related to your real estate needs.

Date: _____ Address: _____

# THANKS FOR VISITING! PLEASE SIGN IN

Name: _____ Phone: _____

Email: _____

Favorite home feature: _____

Recommended Improvements: _____

Price Opinion: _____

How did you learn about this open house? _____

O Newspaper  O Sign  O Real Estate Agent  O Internet          O Other

Is this your first visit?                    O Yes  O No

Do you have a Realtor?  O Yes (what is his name?) _____          O No

Are you pre-qualified/pre-approved to buy a home?          O Yes  O No

What is your time frame for purchasing a new home? ONow OJust looking OWithin a year

Do you have a home to sell?                    O Yes  O No

Do you want us to contact you?                 O Yes  O No

Please list any special needs or comments: _____

_____

Thank you for registering! Disclaimer: We will only send information related to your real estate needs.

---

Name: _____ Phone: _____

Email: _____

Favorite home feature: _____

Recommended Improvements: _____

Price Opinion: _____

How did you learn about this open house? _____

O Newspaper  O Sign  O Real Estate Agent  O Internet          O Other

Is this your first visit?                    O Yes  O No

Do you have a Realtor?  O Yes (what is his name?) _____          O No

Are you pre-qualified/pre-approved to buy a home?          O Yes  O No

What is your time frame for purchasing a new home? ONow OJust looking OWithin a year

Do you have a home to sell?                    O Yes  O No

Do you want us to contact you?                 O Yes  O No

Please list any special needs or comments: _____

_____

Thank you for registering! Disclaimer: We will only send information related to your real estate needs.

Date: _____ Address: _____

# THANKS FOR VISITING! PLEASE SIGN IN

Name: _____ Phone: _____

Email: _____

Favorite home feature: _____

Recommended Improvements: _____

Price Opinion: _____

How did you learn about this open house? _____

O Newspaper  O Sign  O Real Estate Agent  O Internet          O Other

Is this your first visit?                          O Yes  O No

Do you have a Realtor?  O Yes (what is his name?) _____  O No

Are you pre-qualified/pre-approved to buy a home?     O Yes  O No

What is your time frame for purchasing a new home? ONow OJust looking OWithin a year

Do you have a home to sell?                          O Yes  O No

Do you want us to contact you?                       O Yes  O No

Please list any special needs or comments: _____

_____

Thank you for registering! Disclaimer: We will only send information related to your real estate needs.

Name: _____ Phone: _____

Email: _____

Favorite home feature: _____

Recommended Improvements: _____

Price Opinion: _____

How did you learn about this open house? _____

O Newspaper  O Sign  O Real Estate Agent  O Internet          O Other

Is this your first visit?                          O Yes  O No

Do you have a Realtor?  O Yes (what is his name?) _____  O No

Are you pre-qualified/pre-approved to buy a home?     O Yes  O No

What is your time frame for purchasing a new home? ONow OJust looking OWithin a year

Do you have a home to sell?                          O Yes  O No

Do you want us to contact you?                       O Yes  O No

Please list any special needs or comments: _____

_____

Thank you for registering! Disclaimer: We will only send information related to your real estate needs.

Date: _____ Address: _____

# THANKS FOR VISITING! PLEASE SIGN IN

Name: _____ Phone: _____

Email: _____

Favorite home feature: _____

Recommended Improvements: _____

Price Opinion: _____

How did you learn about this open house? _____

O Newspaper  O Sign  O Real Estate Agent  O Internet          O Other

Is this your first visit?                              O Yes  O No

Do you have a Realtor?  O Yes (what is his name?)                    O No

Are you pre-qualified/pre-approved to buy a home?          O Yes  O No

What is your time frame for purchasing a new home? ONow OJust looking OWithin a year

Do you have a home to sell?                          O Yes  O No

Do you want us to contact you?                       O Yes  O No

Please list any special needs or comments: _____

_____

Thank you for registering! Disclaimer: We will only send information related to your real estate needs.

---

Name: _____ Phone: _____

Email: _____

Favorite home feature: _____

Recommended Improvements: _____

Price Opinion: _____

How did you learn about this open house? _____

O Newspaper  O Sign  O Real Estate Agent  O Internet          O Other

Is this your first visit?                              O Yes  O No

Do you have a Realtor?  O Yes (what is his name?)                    O No

Are you pre-qualified/pre-approved to buy a home?          O Yes  O No

What is your time frame for purchasing a new home? ONow OJust looking OWithin a year

Do you have a home to sell?                          O Yes  O No

Do you want us to contact you?                       O Yes  O No

Please list any special needs or comments: _____

_____

Thank you for registering! Disclaimer: We will only send information related to your real estate needs.

Date: _____ Address: _____

# THANKS FOR VISITING! PLEASE SIGN IN

Name: _____ Phone: _____
Email: _____

Favorite home feature: _____
Recommended Improvements: _____
Price Opinion: _____
How did you learn about this open house? _____
O Newspaper O Sign O Real Estate Agent O Internet          O Other
Is this your first visit?                      O Yes O No
Do you have a Realtor?  O Yes (what is his name?) _____        O No
Are you pre-qualified/pre-approved to buy a home?   O Yes O No
What is your time frame for purchasing a new home? ONow OJust looking OWithin a year
Do you have a home to sell?                    O Yes O No
Do you want us to contact you?                 O Yes O No
Please list any special needs or comments: _____
_____

Thank you for registering! Disclaimer: We will only send information related to your real estate needs.

---

Name: _____ Phone: _____
Email: _____

Favorite home feature: _____
Recommended Improvements: _____
Price Opinion: _____
How did you learn about this open house? _____
O Newspaper O Sign O Real Estate Agent O Internet          O Other
Is this your first visit?                      O Yes O No
Do you have a Realtor?  O Yes (what is his name?) _____        O No
Are you pre-qualified/pre-approved to buy a home?   O Yes O No
What is your time frame for purchasing a new home? ONow OJust looking OWithin a year
Do you have a home to sell?                    O Yes O No
Do you want us to contact you?                 O Yes O No
Please list any special needs or comments: _____
_____

Thank you for registering! Disclaimer: We will only send information related to your real estate needs.

Date: _____ Address: _____

# THANKS FOR VISITING! PLEASE SIGN IN

Name: _____ Phone: _____
Email: _____

Favorite home feature: _____
Recommended Improvements: _____
Price Opinion: _____
How did you learn about this open house? _____
O Newspaper  O Sign  O Real Estate Agent  O Internet           O Other
Is this your first visit?                    O Yes  O No
Do you have a Realtor?  O Yes (what is his name?)              O No
Are you pre-qualified/pre-approved to buy a home?      O Yes  O No
What is your time frame for purchasing a new home? ONow OJust looking OWithin a year
Do you have a home to sell?                   O Yes  O No
Do you want us to contact you?                O Yes  O No
Please list any special needs or comments: _____
_____

Thank you for registering! Disclaimer: We will only send information related to your real estate needs.

Name: _____ Phone: _____
Email: _____

Favorite home feature: _____
Recommended Improvements: _____
Price Opinion: _____
How did you learn about this open house? _____
O Newspaper  O Sign  O Real Estate Agent  O Internet           O Other
Is this your first visit?                    O Yes  O No
Do you have a Realtor?  O Yes (what is his name?)              O No
Are you pre-qualified/pre-approved to buy a home?      O Yes  O No
What is your time frame for purchasing a new home? ONow OJust looking OWithin a year
Do you have a home to sell?                   O Yes  O No
Do you want us to contact you?                O Yes  O No
Please list any special needs or comments: _____
_____

Thank you for registering! Disclaimer: We will only send information related to your real estate needs.

Date: _____ Address: _____

# THANKS FOR VISITING! PLEASE SIGN IN

Name: _____ Phone: _____

Email: _____

Favorite home feature: _____

Recommended Improvements: _____

Price Opinion: _____

How did you learn about this open house? _____

O Newspaper  O Sign  O Real Estate Agent  O Internet          O Other

Is this your first visit?                          O Yes  O No

Do you have a Realtor?  O Yes (what is his name?) _____        O No

Are you pre-qualified/pre-approved to buy a home?        O Yes  O No

What is your time frame for purchasing a new home? ONow OJust looking OWithin a year

Do you have a home to sell?                        O Yes  O No

Do you want us to contact you?                     O Yes  O No

Please list any special needs or comments: _____

_____

Thank you for registering! Disclaimer: We will only send information related to your real estate needs.

Name: _____ Phone: _____

Email: _____

Favorite home feature: _____

Recommended Improvements: _____

Price Opinion: _____

How did you learn about this open house? _____

O Newspaper  O Sign  O Real Estate Agent  O Internet          O Other

Is this your first visit?                          O Yes  O No

Do you have a Realtor?  O Yes (what is his name?) _____        O No

Are you pre-qualified/pre-approved to buy a home?        O Yes  O No

What is your time frame for purchasing a new home? ONow OJust looking OWithin a year

Do you have a home to sell?                        O Yes  O No

Do you want us to contact you?                     O Yes  O No

Please list any special needs or comments: _____

_____

Thank you for registering! Disclaimer: We will only send information related to your real estate needs.

Date: _____    Address: _____

# THANKS FOR VISITING! PLEASE SIGN IN

Name: _____    Phone: _____

Email: _____

Favorite home feature: _____

Recommended Improvements: _____

Price Opinion: _____

How did you learn about this open house? _____

O Newspaper  O Sign  O Real Estate Agent  O Internet                    O Other

Is this your first visit?                              O Yes  O No

Do you have a Realtor?  O Yes (what is his name?) _____           O No

Are you pre-qualified/pre-approved to buy a home?          O Yes  O No

What is your time frame for purchasing a new home? ONow OJust looking OWithin a year

Do you have a home to sell?                               O Yes  O No

Do you want us to contact you?                            O Yes  O No

Please list any special needs or comments: _____

_____

Thank you for registering! Disclaimer: We will only send information related to your real estate needs.

---

Name: _____    Phone: _____

Email: _____

Favorite home feature: _____

Recommended Improvements: _____

Price Opinion: _____

How did you learn about this open house? _____

O Newspaper  O Sign  O Real Estate Agent  O Internet                    O Other

Is this your first visit?                              O Yes  O No

Do you have a Realtor?  O Yes (what is his name?) _____           O No

Are you pre-qualified/pre-approved to buy a home?          O Yes  O No

What is your time frame for purchasing a new home? ONow OJust looking OWithin a year

Do you have a home to sell?                               O Yes  O No

Do you want us to contact you?                            O Yes  O No

Please list any special needs or comments: _____

_____

Thank you for registering! Disclaimer: We will only send information related to your real estate needs.

Date: _____ Address: _____

# THANKS FOR VISITING! PLEASE SIGN IN

Name: _____ Phone: _____

Email: _____

Favorite home feature: _____

Recommended Improvements: _____

Price Opinion: _____

How did you learn about this open house? _____

O Newspaper  O Sign  O Real Estate Agent  O Internet          O Other

Is this your first visit?                    O Yes  O No

Do you have a Realtor?  O Yes (what is his name?) _____  O No

Are you pre-qualified/pre-approved to buy a home?      O Yes  O No

What is your time frame for purchasing a new home? ONow OJust looking OWithin a year

Do you have a home to sell?                   O Yes  O No

Do you want us to contact you?                O Yes  O No

Please list any special needs or comments: _____

_____

Thank you for registering! Disclaimer: We will only send information related to your real estate needs.

Name: _____ Phone: _____

Email: _____

Favorite home feature: _____

Recommended Improvements: _____

Price Opinion: _____

How did you learn about this open house? _____

O Newspaper  O Sign  O Real Estate Agent  O Internet          O Other

Is this your first visit?                    O Yes  O No

Do you have a Realtor?  O Yes (what is his name?) _____  O No

Are you pre-qualified/pre-approved to buy a home?      O Yes  O No

What is your time frame for purchasing a new home? ONow OJust looking OWithin a year

Do you have a home to sell?                   O Yes  O No

Do you want us to contact you?                O Yes  O No

Please list any special needs or comments: _____

_____

Thank you for registering! Disclaimer: We will only send information related to your real estate needs.

Date: _____ Address: _____

# THANKS FOR VISITING! PLEASE SIGN IN

Name: _____ Phone: _____

Email: _____

Favorite home feature: _____

Recommended Improvements: _____

Price Opinion: _____

How did you learn about this open house? _____

O Newspaper  O Sign  O Real Estate Agent  O Internet          O Other

Is this your first visit?                           O Yes  O No

Do you have a Realtor?  O Yes (what is his name?)                    O No

Are you pre-qualified/pre-approved to buy a home?        O Yes  O No

What is your time frame for purchasing a new home? ONow OJust looking OWithin a year

Do you have a home to sell?                         O Yes  O No

Do you want us to contact you?                      O Yes  O No

Please list any special needs or comments: _____

_____

_____

Thank you for registering! Disclaimer: We will only send information related to your real estate needs.

---

Name: _____ Phone: _____

Email: _____

Favorite home feature: _____

Recommended Improvements: _____

Price Opinion: _____

How did you learn about this open house? _____

O Newspaper  O Sign  O Real Estate Agent  O Internet          O Other

Is this your first visit?                           O Yes  O No

Do you have a Realtor?  O Yes (what is his name?)                    O No

Are you pre-qualified/pre-approved to buy a home?        O Yes  O No

What is your time frame for purchasing a new home? ONow OJust looking OWithin a year

Do you have a home to sell?                         O Yes  O No

Do you want us to contact you?                      O Yes  O No

Please list any special needs or comments: _____

_____

_____

Thank you for registering! Disclaimer: We will only send information related to your real estate needs.

Date: _____ Address: _____

# THANKS FOR VISITING! PLEASE SIGN IN

Name: _____ Phone: _____

Email: _____

Favorite home feature: _____

Recommended Improvements: _____

Price Opinion: _____

How did you learn about this open house? _____

O Newspaper O Sign O Real Estate Agent O Internet      O Other

Is this your first visit?      O Yes O No

Do you have a Realtor? O Yes (what is his name?) _____ O No

Are you pre-qualified/pre-approved to buy a home?    O Yes O No

What is your time frame for purchasing a new home? ONow OJust looking OWithin a year

Do you have a home to sell?     O Yes O No

Do you want us to contact you?     O Yes O No

Please list any special needs or comments: _____

_____

Thank you for registering! Disclaimer: We will only send information related to your real estate needs.

---

Name: _____ Phone: _____

Email: _____

Favorite home feature: _____

Recommended Improvements: _____

Price Opinion: _____

How did you learn about this open house? _____

O Newspaper O Sign O Real Estate Agent O Internet      O Other

Is this your first visit?      O Yes O No

Do you have a Realtor? O Yes (what is his name?) _____ O No

Are you pre-qualified/pre-approved to buy a home?    O Yes O No

What is your time frame for purchasing a new home? ONow OJust looking OWithin a year

Do you have a home to sell?     O Yes O No

Do you want us to contact you?     O Yes O No

Please list any special needs or comments: _____

_____

Thank you for registering! Disclaimer: We will only send information related to your real estate needs.

Date: _____  Address: _____

# THANKS FOR VISITING! PLEASE SIGN IN

Name: _____ Phone: _____

Email: _____

Favorite home feature: _____

Recommended Improvements: _____

Price Opinion: _____

How did you learn about this open house? _____

O Newspaper  O Sign  O Real Estate Agent  O Internet                    O Other

Is this your first visit?                              O Yes  O No

Do you have a Realtor?  O Yes (what is his name?) _____ O No

Are you pre-qualified/pre-approved to buy a home?        O Yes  O No

What is your time frame for purchasing a new home? ONow OJust looking OWithin a year

Do you have a home to sell?                            O Yes  O No

Do you want us to contact you?                         O Yes  O No

Please list any special needs or comments: _____

_____

Thank you for registering! Disclaimer: We will only send information related to your real estate needs.

---

Name: _____ Phone: _____

Email: _____

Favorite home feature: _____

Recommended Improvements: _____

Price Opinion: _____

How did you learn about this open house? _____

O Newspaper  O Sign  O Real Estate Agent  O Internet                    O Other

Is this your first visit?                              O Yes  O No

Do you have a Realtor?  O Yes (what is his name?) _____ O No

Are you pre-qualified/pre-approved to buy a home?        O Yes  O No

What is your time frame for purchasing a new home? ONow OJust looking OWithin a year

Do you have a home to sell?                            O Yes  O No

Do you want us to contact you?                         O Yes  O No

Please list any special needs or comments: _____

_____

Thank you for registering! Disclaimer: We will only send information related to your real estate needs.

Date: _____ Address: _____

# THANKS FOR VISITING! PLEASE SIGN IN

Name: _____ Phone: _____

Email: _____

Favorite home feature: _____

Recommended Improvements: _____

Price Opinion: _____

How did you learn about this open house? _____

O Newspaper  O Sign  O Real Estate Agent  O Internet                    O Other

Is this your first visit?                          O Yes  O No

Do you have a Realtor?  O Yes (what is his name?)                    O No

Are you pre-qualified/pre-approved to buy a home?        O Yes  O No

What is your time frame for purchasing a new home? ONow OJust looking OWithin a year

Do you have a home to sell?                          O Yes  O No

Do you want us to contact you?                       O Yes  O No

Please list any special needs or comments: _____

_____

_____

Thank you for registering! Disclaimer: We will only send information related to your real estate needs.

---

Name: _____ Phone: _____

Email: _____

Favorite home feature: _____

Recommended Improvements: _____

Price Opinion: _____

How did you learn about this open house? _____

O Newspaper  O Sign  O Real Estate Agent  O Internet                    O Other

Is this your first visit?                          O Yes  O No

Do you have a Realtor?  O Yes (what is his name?)                    O No

Are you pre-qualified/pre-approved to buy a home?        O Yes  O No

What is your time frame for purchasing a new home? ONow OJust looking OWithin a year

Do you have a home to sell?                          O Yes  O No

Do you want us to contact you?                       O Yes  O No

Please list any special needs or comments: _____

_____

_____

Thank you for registering! Disclaimer: We will only send information related to your real estate needs.

Date: _____ Address: _____

# THANKS FOR VISITING! PLEASE SIGN IN

Name: _____ Phone: _____

Email: _____

Favorite home feature: _____

Recommended Improvements: _____

Price Opinion: _____

How did you learn about this open house? _____

O Newspaper  O Sign  O Real Estate Agent  O Internet                    O Other

Is this your first visit?                              O Yes  O No

Do you have a Realtor?  O Yes (what is his name?)                         O No

Are you pre-qualified/pre-approved to buy a home?        O Yes  O No

What is your time frame for purchasing a new home? ONow OJust looking OWithin a year

Do you have a home to sell?                              O Yes  O No

Do you want us to contact you?                           O Yes  O No

Please list any special needs or comments: _____

_____

Thank you for registering! Disclaimer: We will only send information related to your real estate needs.

---

Name: _____ Phone: _____

Email: _____

Favorite home feature: _____

Recommended Improvements: _____

Price Opinion: _____

How did you learn about this open house? _____

O Newspaper  O Sign  O Real Estate Agent  O Internet                    O Other

Is this your first visit?                              O Yes  O No

Do you have a Realtor?  O Yes (what is his name?)                         O No

Are you pre-qualified/pre-approved to buy a home?        O Yes  O No

What is your time frame for purchasing a new home? ONow OJust looking OWithin a year

Do you have a home to sell?                              O Yes  O No

Do you want us to contact you?                           O Yes  O No

Please list any special needs or comments: _____

_____

Thank you for registering! Disclaimer: We will only send information related to your real estate needs.

Date: _____ Address: _____

# THANKS FOR VISITING! PLEASE SIGN IN

Name: _____ Phone: _____

Email: _____

Favorite home feature: _____

Recommended Improvements: _____

Price Opinion: _____

How did you learn about this open house? _____

O Newspaper  O Sign  O Real Estate Agent  O Internet              O Other

Is this your first visit?                              O Yes  O No

Do you have a Realtor?  O Yes (what is his name?) _____        O No

Are you pre-qualified/pre-approved to buy a home?      O Yes  O No

What is your time frame for purchasing a new home?  ONow  OJust looking  OWithin a year

Do you have a home to sell?                           O Yes  O No

Do you want us to contact you?                        O Yes  O No

Please list any special needs or comments: _____

_____

Thank you for registering! Disclaimer: We will only send information related to your real estate needs.

---

Name: _____ Phone: _____

Email: _____

Favorite home feature: _____

Recommended Improvements: _____

Price Opinion: _____

How did you learn about this open house? _____

O Newspaper  O Sign  O Real Estate Agent  O Internet              O Other

Is this your first visit?                              O Yes  O No

Do you have a Realtor?  O Yes (what is his name?) _____        O No

Are you pre-qualified/pre-approved to buy a home?      O Yes  O No

What is your time frame for purchasing a new home?  ONow  OJust looking  OWithin a year

Do you have a home to sell?                           O Yes  O No

Do you want us to contact you?                        O Yes  O No

Please list any special needs or comments: _____

_____

Thank you for registering! Disclaimer: We will only send information related to your real estate needs.

Date: _____  Address: _____

# THANKS FOR VISITING! PLEASE SIGN IN

Name: _____ Phone: _____

Email: _____

Favorite home feature: _____

Recommended Improvements: _____

Price Opinion: _____

How did you learn about this open house? _____

O Newspaper  O Sign  O Real Estate Agent  O Internet          O Other

Is this your first visit?                              O Yes  O No

Do you have a Realtor?  O Yes (what is his name?) _____   O No

Are you pre-qualified/pre-approved to buy a home?        O Yes  O No

What is your time frame for purchasing a new home? ONow OJust looking OWithin a year

Do you have a home to sell?                             O Yes  O No

Do you want us to contact you?                          O Yes  O No

Please list any special needs or comments: _____

_____

Thank you for registering! Disclaimer: We will only send information related to your real estate needs.

---

Name: _____ Phone: _____

Email: _____

Favorite home feature: _____

Recommended Improvements: _____

Price Opinion: _____

How did you learn about this open house? _____

O Newspaper  O Sign  O Real Estate Agent  O Internet          O Other

Is this your first visit?                              O Yes  O No

Do you have a Realtor?  O Yes (what is his name?) _____   O No

Are you pre-qualified/pre-approved to buy a home?        O Yes  O No

What is your time frame for purchasing a new home? ONow OJust looking OWithin a year

Do you have a home to sell?                             O Yes  O No

Do you want us to contact you?                          O Yes  O No

Please list any special needs or comments: _____

_____

Thank you for registering! Disclaimer: We will only send information related to your real estate needs.

Date: _____ Address: _____

# THANKS FOR VISITING! PLEASE SIGN IN

Name: _____ Phone: _____

Email: _____

Favorite home feature: _____

Recommended Improvements: _____

Price Opinion: _____

How did you learn about this open house? _____

O Newspaper  O Sign  O Real Estate Agent  O Internet          O Other

Is this your first visit?                          O Yes  O No

Do you have a Realtor?  O Yes (what is his name?) _____  O No

Are you pre-qualified/pre-approved to buy a home?          O Yes  O No

What is your time frame for purchasing a new home? ONow OJust looking OWithin a year

Do you have a home to sell?                        O Yes  O No

Do you want us to contact you?                     O Yes  O No

Please list any special needs or comments: _____

_____

Thank you for registering! Disclaimer: We will only send information related to your real estate needs.

---

Name: _____ Phone: _____

Email: _____

Favorite home feature: _____

Recommended Improvements: _____

Price Opinion: _____

How did you learn about this open house? _____

O Newspaper  O Sign  O Real Estate Agent  O Internet          O Other

Is this your first visit?                          O Yes  O No

Do you have a Realtor?  O Yes (what is his name?) _____  O No

Are you pre-qualified/pre-approved to buy a home?          O Yes  O No

What is your time frame for purchasing a new home? ONow OJust looking OWithin a year

Do you have a home to sell?                        O Yes  O No

Do you want us to contact you?                     O Yes  O No

Please list any special needs or comments: _____

_____

Thank you for registering! Disclaimer: We will only send information related to your real estate needs.

Date: _____ Address: _____

# THANKS FOR VISITING! PLEASE SIGN IN

Name: _____ Phone: _____

Email: _____

Favorite home feature: _____

Recommended Improvements: _____

Price Opinion: _____

How did you learn about this open house? _____

O Newspaper  O Sign  O Real Estate Agent  O Internet                    O Other

Is this your first visit?                              O Yes  O No

Do you have a Realtor?  O Yes (what is his name?) _____      O No

Are you pre-qualified/pre-approved to buy a home?          O Yes  O No

What is your time frame for purchasing a new home? ONow OJust looking OWithin a year

Do you have a home to sell?                          O Yes  O No

Do you want us to contact you?                       O Yes  O No

Please list any special needs or comments: _____

_____

Thank you for registering! Disclaimer: We will only send information related to your real estate needs.

---

Name: _____ Phone: _____

Email: _____

Favorite home feature: _____

Recommended Improvements: _____

Price Opinion: _____

How did you learn about this open house? _____

O Newspaper  O Sign  O Real Estate Agent  O Internet                    O Other

Is this your first visit?                              O Yes  O No

Do you have a Realtor?  O Yes (what is his name?) _____      O No

Are you pre-qualified/pre-approved to buy a home?          O Yes  O No

What is your time frame for purchasing a new home? ONow OJust looking OWithin a year

Do you have a home to sell?                          O Yes  O No

Do you want us to contact you?                       O Yes  O No

Please list any special needs or comments: _____

_____

Thank you for registering! Disclaimer: We will only send information related to your real estate needs.

Date: _____  Address: _____

# THANKS FOR VISITING! PLEASE SIGN IN

Name: _____  Phone: _____

Email: _____

Favorite home feature: _____

Recommended Improvements: _____

Price Opinion: _____

How did you learn about this open house? _____

O Newspaper  O Sign  O Real Estate Agent  O Internet            O Other

Is this your first visit?                        O Yes  O No

Do you have a Realtor?  O Yes (what is his name?) _____  O No

Are you pre-qualified/pre-approved to buy a home?     O Yes  O No

What is your time frame for purchasing a new home? ONow OJust looking OWithin a year

Do you have a home to sell?                      O Yes  O No

Do you want us to contact you?                   O Yes  O No

Please list any special needs or comments: _____

_____

Thank you for registering! Disclaimer: We will only send information related to your real estate needs.

---

Name: _____  Phone: _____

Email: _____

Favorite home feature: _____

Recommended Improvements: _____

Price Opinion: _____

How did you learn about this open house? _____

O Newspaper  O Sign  O Real Estate Agent  O Internet            O Other

Is this your first visit?                        O Yes  O No

Do you have a Realtor?  O Yes (what is his name?) _____  O No

Are you pre-qualified/pre-approved to buy a home?     O Yes  O No

What is your time frame for purchasing a new home? ONow OJust looking OWithin a year

Do you have a home to sell?                      O Yes  O No

Do you want us to contact you?                   O Yes  O No

Please list any special needs or comments: _____

_____

Thank you for registering! Disclaimer: We will only send information related to your real estate needs.

Date: _____  Address: _____

# THANKS FOR VISITING! PLEASE SIGN IN

Name: _____  Phone: _____

Email: _____

Favorite home feature: _____

Recommended Improvements: _____

Price Opinion: _____

How did you learn about this open house? _____

O Newspaper  O Sign  O Real Estate Agent  O Internet          O Other

Is this your first visit?                              O Yes  O No

Do you have a Realtor?  O Yes (what is his name?) _____        O No

Are you pre-qualified/pre-approved to buy a home?     O Yes  O No

What is your time frame for purchasing a new home?  ONow  OJust looking  OWithin a year

Do you have a home to sell?                           O Yes  O No

Do you want us to contact you?                        O Yes  O No

Please list any special needs or comments: _____

_____

Thank you for registering! Disclaimer: We will only send information related to your real estate needs.

Name: _____  Phone: _____

Email: _____

Favorite home feature: _____

Recommended Improvements: _____

Price Opinion: _____

How did you learn about this open house? _____

O Newspaper  O Sign  O Real Estate Agent  O Internet          O Other

Is this your first visit?                              O Yes  O No

Do you have a Realtor?  O Yes (what is his name?) _____        O No

Are you pre-qualified/pre-approved to buy a home?     O Yes  O No

What is your time frame for purchasing a new home?  ONow  OJust looking  OWithin a year

Do you have a home to sell?                           O Yes  O No

Do you want us to contact you?                        O Yes  O No

Please list any special needs or comments: _____

_____

Thank you for registering! Disclaimer: We will only send information related to your real estate needs.

Date: _____ Address: _____

# THANKS FOR VISITING! PLEASE SIGN IN

Name: _____ Phone: _____

Email: _____

Favorite home feature: _____

Recommended Improvements: _____

Price Opinion: _____

How did you learn about this open house? _____

O Newspaper  O Sign  O Real Estate Agent  O Internet          O Other

Is this your first visit?                         O Yes  O No

Do you have a Realtor?  O Yes (what is his name?) _____          O No

Are you pre-qualified/pre-approved to buy a home?      O Yes  O No

What is your time frame for purchasing a new home? ONow OJust looking OWithin a year

Do you have a home to sell?                       O Yes  O No

Do you want us to contact you?                    O Yes  O No

Please list any special needs or comments: _____

_____

Thank you for registering! Disclaimer: We will only send information related to your real estate needs.

---

Name: _____ Phone: _____

Email: _____

Favorite home feature: _____

Recommended Improvements: _____

Price Opinion: _____

How did you learn about this open house? _____

O Newspaper  O Sign  O Real Estate Agent  O Internet          O Other

Is this your first visit?                         O Yes  O No

Do you have a Realtor?  O Yes (what is his name?) _____          O No

Are you pre-qualified/pre-approved to buy a home?      O Yes  O No

What is your time frame for purchasing a new home? ONow OJust looking OWithin a year

Do you have a home to sell?                       O Yes  O No

Do you want us to contact you?                    O Yes  O No

Please list any special needs or comments: _____

_____

Thank you for registering! Disclaimer: We will only send information related to your real estate needs.

Date: _____ Address: _____

# THANKS FOR VISITING! PLEASE SIGN IN

Name: _____ Phone: _____

Email: _____

Favorite home feature: _____

Recommended Improvements: _____

Price Opinion: _____

How did you learn about this open house? _____

O Newspaper  O Sign  O Real Estate Agent  O Internet                O Other

Is this your first visit?                              O Yes  O No

Do you have a Realtor?  O Yes (what is his name?) _____        O No

Are you pre-qualified/pre-approved to buy a home?        O Yes  O No

What is your time frame for purchasing a new home? ONow OJust looking OWithin a year

Do you have a home to sell?                         O Yes  O No

Do you want us to contact you?                      O Yes  O No

Please list any special needs or comments: _____

_____

Thank you for registering! Disclaimer: We will only send information related to your real estate needs.

Name: _____ Phone: _____

Email: _____

Favorite home feature: _____

Recommended Improvements: _____

Price Opinion: _____

How did you learn about this open house? _____

O Newspaper  O Sign  O Real Estate Agent  O Internet                O Other

Is this your first visit?                              O Yes  O No

Do you have a Realtor?  O Yes (what is his name?) _____        O No

Are you pre-qualified/pre-approved to buy a home?        O Yes  O No

What is your time frame for purchasing a new home? ONow OJust looking OWithin a year

Do you have a home to sell?                         O Yes  O No

Do you want us to contact you?                      O Yes  O No

Please list any special needs or comments: _____

_____

Thank you for registering! Disclaimer: We will only send information related to your real estate needs.

Date: _____  Address: _____

# THANKS FOR VISITING! PLEASE SIGN IN

Name: _____  Phone: _____

Email: _____

Favorite home feature: _____

Recommended Improvements: _____

Price Opinion: _____

How did you learn about this open house? _____

O Newspaper  O Sign  O Real Estate Agent  O Internet              O Other

Is this your first visit?                          O Yes  O No

Do you have a Realtor?  O Yes (what is his name?) _____      O No

Are you pre-qualified/pre-approved to buy a home?        O Yes  O No

What is your time frame for purchasing a new home?  ONow  OJust looking  OWithin a year

Do you have a home to sell?                        O Yes  O No

Do you want us to contact you?                     O Yes  O No

Please list any special needs or comments: _____

_____

Thank you for registering! Disclaimer: We will only send information related to your real estate needs.

---

Name: _____  Phone: _____

Email: _____

Favorite home feature: _____

Recommended Improvements: _____

Price Opinion: _____

How did you learn about this open house? _____

O Newspaper  O Sign  O Real Estate Agent  O Internet              O Other

Is this your first visit?                          O Yes  O No

Do you have a Realtor?  O Yes (what is his name?) _____      O No

Are you pre-qualified/pre-approved to buy a home?        O Yes  O No

What is your time frame for purchasing a new home?  ONow  OJust looking  OWithin a year

Do you have a home to sell?                        O Yes  O No

Do you want us to contact you?                     O Yes  O No

Please list any special needs or comments: _____

_____

Thank you for registering! Disclaimer: We will only send information related to your real estate needs.

Date: _____   Address: _____

# THANKS FOR VISITING! PLEASE SIGN IN

Name: _____   Phone: _____

Email: _____

Favorite home feature: _____

Recommended Improvements: _____

Price Opinion: _____

How did you learn about this open house? _____

O Newspaper  O Sign  O Real Estate Agent  O Internet          O Other

Is this your first visit?                          O Yes  O No

Do you have a Realtor?  O Yes (what is his name?)              O No

Are you pre-qualified/pre-approved to buy a home?        O Yes  O No

What is your time frame for purchasing a new home?  ONow  OJust looking  OWithin a year

Do you have a home to sell?                         O Yes  O No

Do you want us to contact you?                      O Yes  O No

Please list any special needs or comments: _____

_____

Thank you for registering! Disclaimer: We will only send information related to your real estate needs.

---

Name: _____   Phone: _____

Email: _____

Favorite home feature: _____

Recommended Improvements: _____

Price Opinion: _____

How did you learn about this open house? _____

O Newspaper  O Sign  O Real Estate Agent  O Internet          O Other

Is this your first visit?                          O Yes  O No

Do you have a Realtor?  O Yes (what is his name?)              O No

Are you pre-qualified/pre-approved to buy a home?        O Yes  O No

What is your time frame for purchasing a new home?  ONow  OJust looking  OWithin a year

Do you have a home to sell?                         O Yes  O No

Do you want us to contact you?                      O Yes  O No

Please list any special needs or comments: _____

_____

Thank you for registering! Disclaimer: We will only send information related to your real estate needs.

Made in the USA
Las Vegas, NV
06 December 2023

82240736R00059